SHAKESPEARE IN THE CLASSROOM

Open University Press

English, Language, and Education series

General Editor: Anthony Adams
Lecturer in Education, University of Cambridge

SELECTED TITLES IN THE SERIES

The Problem with Poetry
Richard Andrews

Writing Development
Roslyn Arnold

Writing Policy in Action
Eve Bearne and Cath Farrow

Secondary Worlds
Michael Benton

Time for Drama
Roma Burgess and Pamela Gaudry

Thinking Through English
Paddy Creber

Developing Response to Poetry
Patrick Dias and Michael Hayhoe

Developing English
Peter Dougill (ed.)

The Primary Language Book
Peter Dougill and Richard Knott

Children Talk About Books
Donald Fry

English at the Core
Peter Griffith

Literary Theory and English Teaching
Peter Griffith

Lesbian and Gay Issues in the English Classroom
Simon Harris

Reading and Response
Mike Hayhoe and Stephen Parker (eds)

Assessing English
Brian Johnston

Lipservice: The Story of Talk in Schools
Pat Jones

Language and the English Curriculum
John Keen

Shakespeare in the Classroom
Susan Leach

Oracy Matters
Margaret MacLure, Terry Phillips and Andrew Wilkinson (eds)

Language Awareness for Teachers
Bill Mittins

Beginning Writing
John Nichols *et al.*

Teaching Literature for Examinations
Robert Protherough

Developing Response to Fiction
Robert Protherough

The Making of English Teachers
Robert Protherough and Judith Atkinson

Young People Reading
Charles Sarland

English Teaching from A–Z
Wayne Sawyer, Anthony Adams and Ken Watson

Reconstructing 'A' Level English
Patrick Scott

School Writing
Yanina Sheeran and Douglas Barnes

Reading Narrative as Literature
Andrew Stibbs

Collaboration and Writing
Morag Styles (ed.)

Reading Within and Beyond the Classroom
Dan Taverner

Reading for Real
Barrie Wade (ed.)

English Teaching in Perspective
Ken Watson

The Quality of Writing
Andrew Wilkinson

The Writing of Writing
Andrew Wilkinson (ed.)

Spoken English Illuminated
Andrew Wilkinson, Alan Davies and Deborah Berrill

SHAKESPEARE IN THE CLASSROOM

What's the matter?

Susan Leach

Open University Press
Buckingham ● *Philadelphia*

301.034

Open University Press
Celtic Court
22 Ballmoor
Buckingham
MK18 1XW

and
1900 Frost Road, Suite 101
Bristol, PA 19007, USA

First Published 1992

British Library Cataloguing-in-Publication Data

Leach, Susan
  Shakespeare in the classroom?: What's the matter?.
    – (English, language, and education)
  I. Title   II. Series
  822.3

  ISBN 0-335-09674-3

Library of Congress Cataloging-in-Publication Data

Leach, Susan, 1943–
    Shakespeare in the classroom: what's the matter/Susan Leach.
      p.   cm. – (English, language, and education)
    Includes bibliographical references (p.   ) and index.
    ISBN 0-335-09674-3
    1. Shakespeare, William, 1564–1616 – Study and teaching (Primary) –
  Great Britain.   2. Shakespeare, William, 1564–1616 – Study and
  teaching (Secondary) – Great Britain.   3. Drama in education.
  I. Title.   II. Series.
  PR2987.L8   1992
  822.3'3 – dc20   91-33755
                                                          CIP

Typeset by Graphicraft Typesetters Ltd, Hong Kong
Printed in Great Britain by St Edmundsbury Press Ltd
Bury St Edmunds, Suffolk

Contents

Acknowledgements

My thanks are due to Professor Brian Cox, John Edward Taylor Professor of English Literature at Manchester University, for kindly agreeing to give an interview, and for receiving me so hospitably. I would also like to thank Margaret Brown, Head of English at Weobley Comprehensive School, Herefordshire, for permission to use her story 'Oliver and Malovio' in Chapter 8. Above all, my gratitude is due to Dr Rex Gibson, Cambridge Institute of Education, for all his work with the 'Shakespeare in Schools' Project, without which I would never have learnt all that I know.

General editor's introduction

At the time I write (Summer 1991) two versions of the British £20 note are in circulation. One, the larger, has a picture of William Shakespeare on its obverse side; the other, much smaller (the new version), has substituted the scientist, Michael Faraday, for Shakespeare. There seems something peculiarly symbolic in this substitution. The prevailing mood, in a time of economic recession, is more concerned with practical affairs than with drama and the arts as a whole. The introduction in England and Wales of a National Curriculum seems to be leading to an ever-greater marginalization of the arts in education and a greater concentration of time and effort on what can be measured, what has instant observable value in terms of the 'economics of the market-place'. Even the children in the schools have ceased to be, in much of the language of officialdom, 'children' and have become instead 'age weighted pupil units', depending upon how much they contribute to their school's capitation allowance.

In this grim, Gradgrindian context it seems ironic that, as the National Curriculum in English was being established, the one compulsory named author whom all British schoolchildren have to engage with should be the very William Shakespeare, shortly to be demoted from his position of primacy on our currency.

There are several reasons for this. Probably the main one, though also the least important, except symbolically, is the status of Shakespeare as a cultural icon. It is an accident of history, or myth, that he was born and died on 23 April, which also happens to be St George's Day. But this, together with many of the received and remembered representations of Shakespeare, probably most significantly Olivier's wartime film performance of Henry V, means that, in many eyes (even of those who have never read him or seen the plays), Shakespeare and England have taken on a curious sense of corporate identity. This fits, too, the mood of our 'new' Elizabethan age when there is a tendency to look back to the time of Elizabeth I as a time of glory when Britain was still a force to be reckoned with, when Albion was able to defeat the might of Spain and its Armada.

SHAKESPEARE IN THE CLASSROOM

The above has been written very much with a sense of irony but it is not far from the truth as it is seen by many people. Thus, within the last few months, that self-confessed romantic, Prince Charles, has spoken out, on St George's Day itself, about the lack of Shakespeare being taught in schools, claiming that he found it 'almost incredible that in Shakespeare's land one child in seven left school functionally illiterate', though, even if the latter claim is true (which is by no means indisputable), the connection between the two parts of the argument seems tenuous to say the least.

Nonetheless the Prince's speech led to immense media coverage, including four pages of articles in *The Sunday Times* (28 April 1991) attacking the iniquities of 'the progressive elite that has dominated educational thinking for a generation'. It also provided an opportunity for an intervention by the Secretary of State for Education and Science, Mr Kenneth Clarke, who, writing in *The Guardian* (26 April 1991), commented:

> Prince Charles is correct when he asserts that we do not know how much Shakespeare is currently taught. We don't, and we won't until 1992 when that part of the English curriculum comes into play. At 14 we will be sure that every child will be studying at least one or two Shakespeare plays.

Shakespeare has become by now not just an icon but one that is capable of working miracles as Clarke, like the Prince, makes a clear link in his thinking between the 'study' of Shakespeare and achievement in basic literacy.

No doubt goaded on by the inanities of this totally artificial controversy, the then Chair of the National Association for the Teaching of English characterized much teaching of Shakespeare as 'arse-achingly boring' and, earlier, Stephen Spender (who has made his own major contribution to English literature) wrote in *The Independent* Magazine (3 November 1990) that 'the study of Keats and Coleridge, Jane Austen and Shakespeare no longer provides a standard of absolute correctness for students'. This he said, 'does not mean that they should not be studied. It means only that it should be realised that they provide the standard of a great literary tradition which is growing ever-further away from the present, very fluid, Anglo-American language'. (Typically Spender's very well reasoned and restrained article had been headed by the magazine's sub-editor with the provocative, and highly misleading, title: 'Stephen Spender consigns Shakespeare to the past'.)

But the point he makes about our 'present, very fluid, Anglo-American language' lies at the heart of the current debate. Like so much in educational debate today, Shakespeare has become politicized, part of the little Englander's stand against the growing sense of Europeanism, the bulwark protecting the language and the culture of the past against the increasing barbarianism of the present.

It was against the background of this very public debate that the present volume was written. Its author, Susan Leach, is a classroom teacher and Head of an English department, with whom I have had the pleasure of working over many years. In Part One of the book she has made her own observations on the good and the bad reasons for claiming a unique place for Shakespeare in the classroom but it is unlikely that her views would particularly commend themselves either to Prince Charles or to Kenneth Clarke. Much of the argument of the book is that it is precisely the concept of Shakespeare as 'cultural icon' that forms a barrier between his work and a new generation of young people who might otherwise enjoy him.

The book grows, in part, out of Susan's own experience of the Shakespeare in Schools Project, directed over several years by Rex Gibson of the Cambridge Institute of Education. Although her ideas go much further than being simply influenced by Gibson's work (and there may well be some important differences), there is a full acknowledgement of the importance of that project, which worked with hundreds of teachers from all over the British Isles, in the process of the renewal of the teaching of Shakespeare in schools. Prince Charles may not know how much Shakespeare is being taught in schools; my own observation suggests that a combination of Rex Gibson's work and the National Curriculum prescriptions has led to a good deal more than there has been for a long time. One particularly encouraging feature of this has been the growth of the teaching of Shakespeare in primary schools and both the Project's Newsletter ('Shakespeare in Schools') and Susan's Chapter 9 in the present volume exemplify what good practice in this area might entail.

In addition to the work of Rex Gibson there have been other sources of the revival of Shakespeare in schools. Much excellent work has been done in this respect by both the Royal Shakespeare Company and the National Theatre and Susan Leach herself was on secondment for a year from her teaching post completing a Master's degree at the University of Birmingham. Much of her concern at that time was to work on approaches to Shakespeare that could be used in an ordinary classroom with very little space available and the strong sense of classroom reality in the present volume owes much to her work on this.

The key-note throughout is on bringing Shakespeare to life for the present, to release it from a kind of embalmment that has often afflicted it in the past. Thus there is a stress on enactive ways of working with the text and Chapter 7 in particular shows how the processes of deconstruction can enhance our understanding of the texts. But the unique feature of this book is its awareness that just having 'a jolly time' with the text will not do. There needs to be a clear understanding by the teacher of his or her interpretation of the 'book' (to use the stage term from the Elizabethan playhouse that neatly gets us out of the script/text dilemma) and a willing openness to explore that interpretation alongside the interpretations of the class. The 'teaching' of Shakespeare becomes a matter of collaborative exploration, hence the frequent insistence in this book on the circle as the preferred way of working with students of whatever age since it 'deconstructs' the traditional position of authority of the teacher. This is to move Shakespeare firmly away from being a 'sacred text'; it is to restore it to the crucible of the workshop.

There are two other features of Susan Leach's book I especially value. The first, on a positive note, is the stress upon the importance of Shakespeare's language. Too much emphasis upon the notion of 'script' can lead to the English teacher becoming a frustrated producer and the class becoming one in which we get ever further away from what Shakespeare actually wrote. My own experience of Susan's workshops has made it clear that this never happens in her way of working whether it be in primary schools or with university postgraduate students.

The second, a more negative but very important feature, is the worries expressed in Chapter 6 about the substitution for 'the book' of the video instead. There is a real danger that in many classrooms after 1992 the 'study' of 'one or two plays' that Mr Clarke expects will actually be the watching, in a totally passive manner, of videos of varying quality and one may doubt whether this will actually achieve much to enhance the quality of English teaching in schools.

Within the last year or two, as I mention above, I have seen a considerable increase of the teaching of Shakespeare in schools. It has to be admitted that, although the intentions are generally good, the outcomes of this teaching are often quite appalling in practice. My observation of students suggests that this is especially true of young teachers who find it difficult to free themselves from the traditions of Shakespeare teaching in which they have themselves been reared. Yet, introduced to the kind of methods described here, they immediately show a welcome sense of relief; perhaps for the first time for years in their academic education Shakespeare has begun to live again.

I have long wanted to include a book on the teaching of Shakespeare in this series and have spent some years looking for the right author. In Susan Leach I think that I have found the author I was looking for. Naturally I hope this book will have a wide readership and I hope that both Prince Charles and Kenneth Clarke may be numbered among the readers. It acts as a corrective to many of the ill-digested ideas that seem fashionable in the media discussion of these important matters at present.

Anthony Adams

PART ONE
The background

1   Why Shakespeare?

Part One of this book is intended to provide some perspectives from which to reassess the position of Shakespeare in our national consciousness and in our education system. This opening chapter is concerned with historical and cultural perspectives, and with analysis of the ways in which historical and cultural factors have contributed to the current status and position of Shakespeare. It may seem a *sine qua non* that Shakespeare should be included in a National Curriculum for English, but if we attempt to look behind this position, and ask the kinds of question that challenge this assumption, it may be possible to arrive at some answers which can give teachers in the classroom a theoretical framework within which to work, and from which to develop in their own thinking and teaching of Shakespeare.

The most obvious of these hitherto unasked questions might be: why Shakespeare? Does it go without saying that this particular English playwright and poet should have become the cultural national icon of the English? Many critics would have it so, and the furore caused by the publication of a book which did indeed ask this question, and attempted to answer it at length,[1] bears witness to the kind of reverence accorded to Shakespeare in the national consciousness. It appears that Shakespeare, like God, is not to be questioned; only this is a particular kind of God, and a particular kind of Shakespeare. The one is God as referred to in a remark attributed to Peter Plouviez, President of the actors' union, Equity: 'Equity welcomes talented foreign artists in our country even when they are required to play such an obviously British part as God'.[2] The other is Shakespeare as referred to by Mr Henry Crawford in *Mansfield Park*: 'Shakespeare one gets aquainted with without knowing how. It is part of an Englishman's constitution. His thoughts and beauties are so spread abroad that one touches them everywhere, one is intimate with him by instinct.'[3] In other words, Shakespeare is like the air we breathe, the food we eat. He gets inside us without our being aware of it. In a culturally unquestioning context, there is no more to be said. Each figurehead carries the stamp of absolute authority, that rightness which fulfils so well the requirements of bourgeois capitalism. If we drop God from the comparison, and focus solely on Shakespeare, we find that only since the 1960s has any serious questioning of Shakespeare and the whole canon of English Literature taken place, and only since that time have critics and theorists articulated radical challenges to these prior assumptions.

To return to the question: why Shakespeare? A satisfactory answer to this question is difficult, largely because it involves a kind of circularity of cause and effect, and the application of comparative and evaluative judgements which belong more properly in the field of aesthetics and literary history. The evaluations made possible by these disciplines are, however, so culture- and class-specific that they are ill placed to provide answers framed within any other set of perspectives. Recent critical practice predicates itself on the *fact* of Shakespeare in his present position, and while observations that draw attention to the *constructed* nature of Shakespeare's status are extremely useful in challenging the assumptions that have accrued around it, they do not attempt to justify or challenge that position by recourse to comparisons with the 'greatness' of any other writer. In the interests of becoming familiar with a kind of deconstructive process which can begin to demonstrate *how* the processes have worked which have put Shakespeare where he is, it is probably more useful to ask the question 'how?' than the question 'why?'

Briefly, Shakespeare has become our National Poet by going through what one might characterize as processes of acculturation: in his own lifetime, and then later after the Restoration, his existence was very much a part of theatrical practice and the theatres' need for successful scripts; gradually he became the subject of interest as reading matter and went through the process of being extensively edited; in the late nineteenth century he became the subject of literary criticism, and became linked to English, English Literature and the notions of nationhood and patriotism which those areas of study increasingly came to express. It is perhaps no coincidence that while Shakespeare's death is known to have occurred on 23 April, his birth has also been attributed to that day, thus neatly wrapping him up in the flag of St George, patron saint of England, whose saint's day is, of course, 23 April. In the process of these reinventions, he has been laden with ever increasing cultural and class value by succeeding generations. In particular, he can be said to have performed certain functions for those people in each generation whose interest it was to make something of him (often for profit), and the uses to which his works have been put increasingly reflect the growth and power of Western capitalism.

For the first part of the construction process, and in addition to the very high esteem in which he was held by his contemporaries,[4] which by itself would not have guaranteed his immortality, it is the history of theatre in the seventeenth century which seems to provide explanations for the increasing predominance of Shakespeare on the English stage. This was not least because closure of the theatres during the Commonwealth deprived any latent playwrights of opportunities to write for a living, and theatre managers of the newly opened theatres of the 1660s were forced to look back to the early years of the century for their material. The history thereafter becomes part of the development of theatres themselves, with actor managers and pre-eminent actors setting a tone and a range of expectations and assumptions about Shakespeare which continue to this day. It was at this time that Shakespeare began to be identified with God: to Dryden he was 'sacred', to various other writers he was 'immortal', 'godlike', 'divine'; to the Earl of Shaftesbury[5] '*Hamlet* seemed to have most affected English hearts', an assessment which conflated Shakespeare with Englishness in a way that reached its apogee in the late nineteenth and early twentieth centuries. It needs to be remembered throughout this brief résumé of his history, that Shakespeare would not have been acted at all if performances of his plays had not been profitable for theatres.

The production of the first collected edition of Shakespeare's plays, the First Folio of 1623, had been undertaken as a labour of love by two friends of Shakespeare, Heminge and Condell, and as a means of recording and preserving the texts. This was editing with a different aim from that informing the second stage of the construction process, which began during the course of the late seventeenth and eighteenth centuries with the 'literalization' of Shakespeare, that is, the production of editions of his works, brought out first by men of the theatre such as Davenant with his version of *Hamlet* for Drury Lane (1661), and then by other poets and writers like Dryden, and later Pope. Even at this stage of the process publishing Shakespeare did not make money: the publisher Jacob Tonson, who only later published a collection of the works of Shakespeare, was in 1695 publishing *The Poetical Works of Mr. John Milton*, an author from whom he made more money in his publishing career than from any other. In other words, Shakespeare at the end of the seventeenth century was by no means regarded as the best writer in English and publishing the collected works would not have been worth risking.

In addition to these developments, account needs to be taken of the developing tastes, spending power and education of the middle classes, of the increase in adult literacy, especially among women, and of the changing nature of capitalism which at this time was busy, as now, in 'commoditifying' what it could lay hands on. The changing nature of social relationships produced by the larger changes in society generally (for example, increasing merchant venturing, colonization, and the rapid growth in trade with the colonies in America based on slaves, sugar and cotton) resulted in a growth in wealth that in itself generated demands for commodities. Plays can be made into commodities in two ways: either by being performed under conditions where ownership and managerial decisions are directed towards profit, or by being published and turned into commodities for a growing and more demanding readership. In the case of Shakespeare, this is increasingly what happened in the last years of the seventeenth century, and throughout the eighteenth century. Under the editorship of Rowe (1709), Pope (1725), Theobald (1733), Warburton (1747), Johnson (1765), and Capell (1768), the plays were edited, annotated, explained, glossed and then, as patterned by each editor, made the subject of critiques, attacks and counter-attacks, where not only Shakespeare but also individual editors came in for obloquy. The process also involved the 'classification' of Shakespeare: that is, in an age when classical models, genre specificity and precision were valued, ways were found to justify Shakespeare as 'classic' although he exhibited quite unclassical characteristics. In relation to Aristotle, for example, he clearly could not be called a 'classical' writer. The words of a hitherto untranslated and rather obscure classical Greek critic called Longinus, who only appeared in English for the first time in 1674, usefully provided the following for those critics who were unhappy about Shakespeare's structural and linguistic weaknesses:

> I readily allow, that Writers of a lofty and tow'ring Genius are by no means pure and correct, since whatever is neat and accurate throughout must be exceedingly liable to Flatness. In the Sublime, as in great Affluence of Fortune, some minuter Articles will unavoidably escape Observation . . . its very height and Grandeur exposes the Sublime to sudden Falls.[6]

The third stage of the construction of Shakespeare is the main contribution of the eighteenth century. For that century, Shakespeare needed rescuing from the darkness of the previous century, and the twin processes of being edited and being turned into a classic also performed the function of turning Shakespeare into reading matter, as opposed to theatrical matter. The internalization of response in the individual which reading, an essentially solitary process, produced, in contrast to the social, celebratory response characteristic of participation in a performance of a play, developed into the kind of private interaction with the plays more typical of the nineteenth century. This kind of response, initially associated with the Romantic poets, is described by them in their diaries and letters – Coleridge in 1828 talks of having 'a smack of Hamlet myself, if I may say so';[7] Keats in his letters (1814–1821) says, 'Hamlet's heart was full of such Misery as mine is when he said to Ophelia "Go to a Nunnery, go, go!" Indeed I should like to give up the matter at once – I should like to die';[8] Byron in 1830 decides, 'We love Hamlet even as we love ourselves' – each of them pointing down one of the paths of the Shakespeare experience that is still being trodden.[9] Self-identification with characters in the plays, quoting of relevant lines out of context as illustrative of some particular frame of mind in the reader, can be seen as part of the process whereby Shakespeare came to be talked of by Henry Crawford in the way quoted above: that is, the words of Shakespeare the playwright, coming more and more to be identified with Shakespeare the man, are seen to permeate the English language and to make possible utterances of a particularly 'beautiful' and apt kind.

Another result of the predominantly solitary engagement with Shakespeare implicit in reading is the kind of response expressed here by William Hazlitt: 'We do not like to see our author's plays acted, and least of all, HAMLET. There is no play that suffers so much in being transferred to the stage. Hamlet himself seems hardly capable of being acted.'[10] Comments like these both encapsulate and make possible the idea of there being a 'real' Hamlet somewhere, which by extension develops into 'real' characters of Shakespeare's plays. Hazlitt continues his remarks by talking of 'the natural grace and refined susceptibility of the character' of Hamlet, thereby highlighting that process of the imagination which occurs in the reader as the words on the page make possible an individual conception of character, and throwing into relief the extraordinary idea that plays are better not acted. The distance travelled since the days of the Globe Theatre is indeed immense – Hazlitt's observations can also be seen as the expression of a process by which the individual is constructed as consumer and the individual response made to take precedence over communal experience.

We have, therefore, at this stage of the processing of Shakespeare, in the early years of the nineteenth century, reached a point where he is read in any one of a number of editions, his characters are beginning to be seen to have a life of their own, a life more obvious to the reader than to the playgoer, where it is quite acceptable for people of standing to condemn the staging of at least one play as unequal to the truths contained within it (Hazlitt, in his comment quoted in the previous paragraph, obviously cannot see the intellectual and interpretative contortions implied by his position but which seem clear enough to us), and where the scene is set for whole worlds of criticism and comment to be produced which entirely ignore Shakespeare as playwright. By the early years of the twentieth century, for example, it was possible for A.C. Bradley to talk about the Tragedies as though they were novels without the authorial voice.[11] The continuation of the process of the bourgeois appropriation of Shakespeare ensured that he would continue to be identified with, and identifiable as, the true expression of nationhood and Englishness as the nineteenth became the twentieth century.

This position has diverged into the multifarious strands of Shakespeare with which we are familiar today. That is, Shakespeare purely as text to be read, as playwright to be acted, as subject matter for examinations, as advertising matter, as hotelkeeper, as street name, as mark of the 'educated' person, as initiator of a tourist industry, as a marker of cultural acceptability, and most pervasively as an integral part of the way English is used: 'we all talk Shakespeare, use his similes, and describe with his descriptions' says Edmund in *Mansfield Park*,[12] and it is rare for a day to pass without some reference to him or use of his language in any of the print or visual media.

The separate but related development during the nineteenth century of English as a subject to be studied, and the parallel growth of concepts and definitions of Englishness, was to a large extent the result of Britain becoming the largest imperial power which had ever existed. The concomitant pressures for an educated class capable of running the necessary bureaucracy produced a need for an educational rationale based on a strong informing idea of British superiority underpinned by appropriate icons. Queen Victoria became constructed as one of these figureheads, although during his life the German Prince

Albert was even more prominent in his extraordinary commitment to Englishness. As the century progressed, bringing with it huge increases in British economic and industrial power, buttressed by the largest navy on earth, the importance of 'greatness' became even more overriding. The term came to be applied to many figures of 'English Literature' – itself a term and a concept first coined in the nineteenth century. By 1875, for example, English as a subject was in existence in the form of language, literature and history, and was already well established in the educational provision for boys, as a group of examination subjects to test eligibility for entry into the Civil Service, the Armed Forces, the professions and the universities. (Girls of the middle and upper classes were not exempt from the experience of English literature, nor from the study of Shakespeare, yet while this reading and study undoubtedly produced widely read, articulate and literate as well as literary women, it had no overtly public purpose or outcome: it was not expected to do more than produce suitable wives and soulmates for the middle- and upper-class males experiencing a male version of the same system.) The educated class required for the running and administration of the British Empire was schooled in the concepts of nationhood which could be read into English Literature, and in the patriotic stance assumed to inhere in the writings of the Great English Poets.

Within this system, Shakespeare and knowledge of Shakespeare became and remained central to ideas of nationhood, the educated man (rather than woman) and social and cultural acceptability. An era of literary criticism began during these latter years of the nineteenth century which shaped and informed responses to Shakespeare in a way that has proved very durable. In the same way that many English middle-class and lower-middle-class cultural and political tastes and attitudes are perceptibly shaped by the residues of nineteenth-century ideology, however different they superficially appear to be, so ideas of greatness in literature, and of Shakespeare in particular, have been dominated by the views of critics who were themselves inescapably products of nineteenth-century imperialism and its painful and challenging twentieth-century aftermath – A.C. Bradley, Sir Walter Raleigh, and John Dover Wilson,[13] among others, and the editors of the time, Greg, Craig and Dowden, who represented the first significant intrusion of academics into the Shakespeare business. The extraordinary language used by these academics in describing Shakespeare tells us a great deal about their own ideology and outlook, but little about Shakespeare. George Saintsbury, Professor of English at Edinburgh, wrote in 1887.

> Everything in him passes, in some mysterious way, under and into that 'species of eternity' which transforms all the great works of art, which at once prevents them from being mere copies of Nature, and excuses whatever there is of nature in them that is not beautiful or noble. . . . But he is always – and this is the extraordinary and almost inexplicable difference, not merely between him and all his contemporaries, but between him and all other writers – at the height of the particular situation.[14]

In spite of Saintsbury's adulation, and in spite of the undoubted popularity of the plays in performance during his own lifetime, the evidence is that for much of the seventeenth century, that is, in the years immediately after his death, Shakespeare was deemed inferior by most critics to John Fletcher and to Ben Jonson. In other words, Saintsbury's 'inexplicable' differences are the result of differences of construction and shaping, and not something that can be defined as intrinsic.

However, Saintsbury was not alone in his adoration: Swinburne's introduction to the Oxford Edition of Shakespeare, first published in 1911, is full of similarly inflated language and hyperbolic assertions:

> The bearer of that name (Shakespeare) was the one supreme creator of men who ever rose among mortals to show them and to leave them with an all but innumerable race of evident and indisputable immortals. No child of man and woman was too high or too low for his perfect apprehension and appreciation. Of good and evil, in all their subtlest and sublimest forms of thought and action and revelation, he knew more than ever it has been given to any other man to know.[15]

This strikes us now as absurd, and again tells us far more about the times in which it was written, particularly the ideology of those times, than it does about Shakespeare. But this kind of idealizing and adulation remains today embedded in the commonly agreed valuations of Shakespeare, and in the currency of language used about him. The attribution to Shakespeare the man of qualities about which we can know nothing, the expressed need to hero-worship, the apparently vital necessity to 'own' the 'best' writer 'the world has ever known', the notions of Shakespeare's universality, have all found their expression in the 1989 National Curriculum for English in England and Wales.[16]

It is important to notice the link between the setting up of English degree courses in British universities in the late nineteenth century and the inclusion of English in national education provision based on explicitly ideological aims on the one hand, and the latest embodiment of Shakespeare as national icon in the National Curriculum for English on the other. By the early 1920s the process was almost complete which placed Shakespeare in a central position not only in universities but also in the national education system. To the extent that a crisis of authority and leadership after the First World War was addressed via the education system, Shakespeare was pressed into service as one means of control. If English literature is constantly reconstructed as a sublime and universal experience, the message conveyed is that those without experience of it are outside the pale. It is sobering to consider how powerfully this cultural domination has worked: there are plenty of people today whose educational and class experiences have already disenfranchised them from participating in any experience of Shakespeare.

This process has also led to the current situation, noticeable in the responses of many 'educated' people to Shakespeare, that there is one correct and proper Shakespeare, who or which exists as an amalgamation of concepts of the man (a large amount of invention has gone into this, as well as the projection of cultural needs – Swinburne, quoted above, is a good example of this), the plays (ideal, Platonic versions of these exist somewhere above the ether to which such adherents have ready access), the characters in the plays (who have become 'real' people and who also have ideal existences somewhere else, possibly in the same land that characters from novels inhabit, but who certainly exist beyond and apart from the plays), and the quality of universality (supported by extensive *hors de texte* quotation, and use of lines and half-lines in a plethora of contexts). This happy combination of separate elements provides a rich source of inspiration for the whole contemporary cultural edifice, from beermats to stately homes.

There is, however, a difference between this position and that which appears to have operated in the nineteenth century and earlier, before the canonization process had really got under way, in spite of bourgeois ambitions to own Shakespeare. This is illustrated by reference to writers like Dickens and Mark Twain, and further back to a largely forgotten eighteenth-century playwright, Aaron Hill, who all regarded Shakespeare in a more sober light. For them, and therefore also for their audiences, and for the particular discourses and ideologies within which they were operating, Shakespeare is not the unchallengeable and fixed entity so desperately sought after in more recent times. For Aaron Hill, for example, Shakespeare provided a model for a new play about Henry V to which the author provided the following Preface *To the Reader*:

> The inimitable, and immortal, Shakespeare, about a hundred and thirty years since, wrote a play, on this subject, and call'd it, The life of King Henry, the Fifth: Mine is a New Fabrick, yet I built on this Foundation; and the Reader, I am afraid, will, too easily, discover, without the Help of a comparison, in what Places I am indebted to him. . . . The success, which this Tragedy will meet with, on the Stage, is a Matter, of no Consequence; If it were otherwise, I shou'd be sorry, to have mistaken, so unseasonably, the Taste of the Fashionable![17]

This play and its production illustrate two attitudes taken in the eighteenth century: turning already existing plays into reading matter was a well-established practice (there is clearly nothing strange about publishing this play as a script to be read before it has ever been tried on the stage); and the use of Shakespeare in a new version, abundantly furnished with the new playwright's own ideas. The play in question can only be said to be *very* distantly related to *Henry V*, dealing as it does with a totally invented young lady called Harriet, the daughter of the dead brother of Lord Scroop (who plays a much more complex and extensive role in this play than in Shakespeare's) who spends much of the play attempting to bring Henry to book for jilting her. In the end, after an impassioned series of speeches to him, and just when he seems on the point of giving way, she stabs herself and is carried off stage. In the London of 1723, a year after the death of the Duke of Marlborough, hero of at least four victories over the French, plays about kingly power misused, promises broken, courtship and marriage are surprisingly as important as anything overtly to do with war and conquest.

Nevertheless, it is *Henry V* which Hill chooses to adapt, and that play is implacably about defeating the French. What Hill's play does is to turn the main concerns of the war with France into questions of emotional and domestic import. Shakespeare's play (incorrectly titled by Hill) surfaces periodically in Hill's text in such lines as:

> Now, All the Youth of England are on Fire,
> And silken Dalliance sleeps in dusty Wardrobes;
> Now, thrive the Armourers: and Honour's Flame
> Burns in the beating Breast of each rous'd Soldier.

Why Aaron Hill felt the compulsion to do this to the play is another matter. The full title of his play is *King Henry the Fifth: OR, The conquest of France, by the English*, an indication that those recent wars were still very much in the cultural foreground. But, the battle of Agincourt does not take place until right at the end of the play, and victory is elaborately signalled by the 'Genius of England', which rises and sings, among other words, the following:

> Hark! Hark! – 'tis done!
>   The Day is won!
> They bend! they break! the fainting Gauls give way!
> And yield, reluctant, to their Victor's Sway!
>   Happy Albion! – strong to gain!
> Let Union teach Thee, not to win, in vain.

It is clear that what Aaron Hill is doing here is using some of Shakespeare to express the ideological needs of his own day: France must be seen to be conquered, and England's newly imposed union with Scotland and the development of patriotic fervour must be celebrated. Hill does this by using this Genius of England, who sings of a mythical Albion which only a few years later (1740) became Britannia, in the most enduring of those eighteenth-century peaens to these islands, 'Rule, Britannia!'.

By the time Dickens was writing, a century later, the embedding of Shakespeare in the national consciousness had reached a much more advanced stage, but also paradoxically appears to have shifted, in class terms, down from Hill's 'fashionable' clientele, and also from Jane Austen's middle-class Crawford, to the lower middle classes and below who formed a large portion of Dickens's reading public. Mr Wopsle's performance as Hamlet, in the Drury Lane theatre which Pip and Herbert visit in *Great Expectations*, depends for its comic effect on a shared understanding and familiarity with the play itself.[18] Dickens is appealing to such a community of experience in a way that goes beyond the ability to quote the surface clichés, and also uses Shakespeare as a referent for status; Mr Wopsle in a sense has 'arrived' in this performance. This paradox, of both familiarity and status, echoing more nearly than anything achievable now the conditions under which Shakespeare existed in the London of Elizabeth and James, is similarly present in *Nicholas Nickleby*.[19] The Crummles' theatrical troupe perform *Romeo and Juliet* in the theatre at Southampton in conditions that are barely practicable, where an illiterate victim of the Yorkshire Schools plays the part of the Apothecary, and a young ingenue with no previous experience plays Romeo, and where it is taken for granted that Shakespeare will take his place alongside other playwrights, including Nicholas himself. What Dickens communicates through this arrangement is Shakespeare as *primus inter pares*, the kind of Shakespeare who has continued to exist in the world of amateur theatre and school productions.

Imbued as he was with the plays and words of Shakespeare, Dickens's novels are full of quotes and half-quotes, unacknowledged by him and usually unnoticed by modern editors, which indicate the actuality of Henry Crawford's statement about Shakespeare getting into you unnoticed. In America, later in the century, brought about by a different but equally effective process, Shakespeare is also a common currency of cultural allusion, so that Mark Twain in *Huckleberry Finn*[20] can assume a readership that will see the absurdity of the duke and the king and their Shakespearean presentation, and that will also see the hilarious nature of the *Hamlet* soliloquy ('the most celebrated thing in Shakespeare') which the duke has to piece together from an obviously imperfect memory, as he has only one volume of the plays with him, which is not the Tragedies.

The processes which have somehow lost this creative, irreverential and celebratory approach to Shakespeare, involving non-professional and non-academic actors, audiences and readers, are partly accounted for by the history of the construction of Shakespeare outlined above. Certainly the appropriation of Shakespeare by the academic establishment, and his subsequent appearance in university English Literature courses and examinations, and then in school examinations (School Certificate and its precursors and successors) has turned him, and perceptions of him, into something that would not have been recognized until the late nineteenth century. Since his death, Shakespeare has been used as an icon for nationalism and greatness for a large part of his subsequent existence, the definitions given to those concepts being culture-specific and time-specific. Only relatively recently have critics begun to challenge the inevitabilty of these processes of iconisation, hitherto taken for granted. They challenge the notion that Shakespeare *is* the greatest ever writer in English, both as playwright and poet, and seek instead to show how this process has occurred, and what it has done to our ideas and expectations of Shakespeare in the process. Meanwhile, Shakespeare, thinly disguised in post-modern clothes, makes his appearance in the National Curriculum for English.

2 Shakespeare in the National Curriculum

Chapter 1 has outlined some of the historical and cultural processes which have produced the multi-faceted Shakespeare we know in the late twentieth century. This chapter addresses itself to the more recent history of developments in the state education system which have resulted in Shakespeare being firmly located in the National Curriculum for English.

Several converging factors are involved here: the wider issue of literature and its perceived role in the curriculum, which will be referred to as appropriate during the chapter; the role of Shakespeare as a subject for study and examination; and the way in which the National Curriculum for English has itself emerged from the recent history of English in schools as a key issue of national debate.

Within the general framework of literature in the classroom, which is a continually evolving and changing component of the English curriculum, shaped to fulfil a variety of sometimes conflicting ideological aims, the status of Shakespeare is unassailable; as Alan Sinfield observes: 'For literary criticism, Shakespeare is the keystone which guarantees the ultimate stability and rightness of the category "Literature"'.[1] In addition to legitimizing the whole literary edifice, Shakespeare also operates as a powerful denoter of class perceptions, and to some extent class position, so that while his position is pre-eminent, the view of it varies according to the outlook of the onlooker. The view from the middle class is undoubtedly more assured and familiar than that from the working class; it is, after all, the middle classes who are now most likely to go to the theatre to see a Shakespeare production. For working-class pupils, and adults, by and large, 'Shakespeare is not for the likes of us'. In many respects this is a deliberately contrived situation, unlike what I have suggested was the position in the nineteenth century. In spite of the felt need to 'civilize' the working classes with literature in the nineteenth century, the dominant ethos now in connection with Shakespeare is one of exclusion.[2]

In spite and perhaps also because of this, both middle-class and working-class pupils in schools are fully alert to the status of Shakespeare, and both refer to the same sense of cultural hierarchy when they say 'Shakespeare's proper literature' and 'Shakespeare's a snob'. In other words, both sets of pupils and therefore, it is fairly safe to say, *all* pupils have imbibed an idea of Shakespeare which sets him above everything else in their perceptions: in one case to be acknowledged and used because of the status conferred by studying 'proper' literature; in the other case to be avoided, because of the 'otherness', the alien and oppressive nature of what he has been made to stand for by the establishment, and by the critical construction put on him. What I want to look at here is the kind of context for Shakespeare that current curricular and examination demands produce, what those demands are now, and what they have been in the past.

According to David Hornbrook,

> Shakespeare for most children is inescapably associated with social snobbery. Perceived (accurately) as the property of a minority of 'academic' children at the top of the school, the literary A stream, the plays carry an elitist tag which excludes them from the legitimate business of a world defined by *Brookside* and *Eastenders*.[3]

Pupils, however, are both excluders and excluded. In status- and class-dominated British society those who have not experienced Shakespeare, and who therefore are not familiar with some of the sayings and 'quotes' which are the mark of the 'educated' person, are further alienated from the cultural establishment, which has, of course, been busy excluding them anyway from birth. The current position of Shakespeare in schools, before the National Curriculum requirements are put into effect, is usefully characterized by David Hornbrook: 'any attempt to chart the location and significance of Shakespeare on the contemporary curriculum is to embark on an ethnography of absence'. This seems a far cry from the position that one might expect. The greatest playwright in the world not being taught in schools! The national icon removed from the niche! What can explain this? The fundamental changes that have taken place in the English education system since the 1944 Education Act are largely the reasons for the current situation: the introduction and establishment of comprehensive schooling; the institution of examinations designed to cater for a far greater proportion of the school population than the old School Certificate; the advent of a succession of Conservative governments, impelled by a 'radical' right-wing ideology, which have shaken the system from top to bottom, imposing such huge requirements on teachers and school time for extra purposes, that it is problematical whether Shakespeare or anyone else will be well served by these new conditions.

Before the 1944 Act, pupils in the already existing high schools, grammar schools and private schools were taught Shakespeare as a matter of course, and, if they were regarded as suitable material, might then be examined on him in School Certificate examinations. Pupils in elementary schools had varied experiences of Shakespeare, but while possibly being among the number celebrating Shakespeare Day,[4] as described by the Newbolt Report of 1921 in terms of high approval, many had no experience of Shakespeare and came to express their own position as quoted above: 'Shakespeare is not for the likes of us'. The situation was very similar to that produced by the introduction of O level examinations in 1951, and can be characterized as an almost entirely class-based experience of Shakespeare: if you went to elementary school, or its later equivalent, the secondary modern school, from which you were ejected into the world at the age of 13 or 14, you probably did not experience Shakespeare; if you went to any other educational establishment, and, in particular, if you went to any school that prepared you for further or higher education, then you almost certainly studied Shakespeare at least up to O level standard.

By the time O level examinations had become established, any idea of a community of experience of Shakespeare was a long way in the past. O levels expanded and built on the pattern of the old School Certificate, but these examinations were designed to serve a changed school clientele. The 1944 Education Act, having laid the foundation for a tripartite system which rested largely in the end on only two of the three originally proposed types of maintained school, the secondary modern and the selective grammar school, did open up to a larger section of the population the opportunities of staying at school to sit qualifying examinations. Even then, with the legal school-leaving age at 14, rising to 15 in 1951, pupils had to make active decisions about remaining in school to sit O levels; whereas this was the norm in grammar schools, it was far less likely in secondary modern schools, and was indeed impossible in many of them where there were no teaching facilities to take pupils into O level studies. Consequently, the class-based nature of exposure to Shakespeare remained part of the system: the larger clientele for O level, as compared to School Certificate, simply ensured that a larger percentage of the top of the ability range in the school population was familiar with some of Shakespeare.

Shakespeare featured in these O level examinations in much the same way as had been the case for School Certificate: one Shakespeare play was studied, along with some poetry (the *Oxford Book of English Verse* was the remembered School Certificate experience of one respondent) and a novel. However, for many pupils the examination text was the culmination of several years of reading and studying Shakespeare in the classroom, in a variety of ways, but usually described as 'traditional', and so the later experience was supported by the earlier work. The questions on Shakespeare on O level papers were not particularly penetrating but demanded more than a superficial familiarity with the texts: '"While we may hope for a happy ending to *King Lear*, Shakespeare's conclusion is entirely fitting." Discuss' (AEB, O level); 'Write about the dramatic effectiveness of the last act of *Twelfth Night*, and show how the ending is connected to earlier episodes in the play' (London, O level).[5] I shall be examining in a later chapter the significance and culturally determined nature of the kind of teaching and experience of the plays which will produce the expected answers to these questions; for now, it is important to reflect that this O level experience of Shakespeare was for many people the only time in their lives when they ever read any of the plays, and it may well be that, in the maintained sector of the state system, O level gave access to Shakespeare to more pupils than anything before or since. (In the private sector, the conditions for the teaching of Shakespeare have tended to be more favourable, and experience of Shakespeare has been regarded as an integral part of the whole 'independent' experience.)

Certainly, the situation produced by the advent in 1965 of the Certificate of Secondary Education (CSE) did not radically alter the incidence of Shakespeare study. The new examination, established as a means of enabling the 40 per cent of the ability range below the O level cohort to leave school with some kind of qualification, had a rather different set of imperatives. It should be pointed out here that this percentage of examinable pupils was purely notional at this time, as the statutory school-leaving age was still 15 and pupils still had to make a conscious decision to stay at school to take examinations set for 16-year-olds. When the school-leaving age was raised to the present 16 years there were potentially more candidates available for CSE examinations. However, these so-called 'Newsom pupils' were not generally those who would find any relevance in Shakespeare, and it is from this point onwards that the systematic absolute decline in Shakespeare in schools can be dated.

From the start CSE was established as a system based on far greater teacher input than was ever the case with O level, and in many instances was run by teachers. They were empowered, where they so chose, to set, mark and finally moderate examinations in English and English Literature. This was quite unlike O level, the administration of which was in the hands of the nine O level boards, eight of which were wholly or partly controlled by universities. The vested interests universities had in preserving the critical status quo, and in ensuring for themselves the steady production of candidates for university English degree courses with the 'right' approach, resulted in the repetitive and relatively static nature of the kinds of question asked, and the setting of the same plays for examination. This control was also the cause of the exclusion of teachers, except the select few, from the examination-setting processes, although they came in very useful for marking the candidates' completed papers.

Teachers involved in the setting of CSE papers, particularly those operating a so-called 'Mode 3', which allowed the whole process to be largely in their control, were able to make choices of their own about the inclusion of Shakespeare, and, given the captive position of many of the pupils for whom they were devising the examinations in the first place, often chose to exclude Shakespeare altogether, in favour of more accessible and 'relevant' material. The CSE boards, which set examinations for English Literature, offered a list of texts, and made very general stipulations, but Shakespeare was never prescribed for study. Apart from examinations, another way of acquiring a qualification in English Literature was by a 100 per cent coursework folder which followed stipulations laid down by the CSE board. Needless to say, Shakespeare was not one of those stipulations.[6]

While these two examinations, O level and CSE, continued to operate side by side, a certain number of pupils continued to experience Shakespeare as part of their English course. O level continued for many years to retain its high status value, and was jealously maintained as the only 'proper' examination in grammar schools, and as a means of selecting pupils for admission to sixth forms. After several dry runs in the shape of 16+ examinations and modifications of CSE courses, in addition to the modifications that were being offered in some O level syllabuses, the General Certificate of Secondary Education (GCSE) at last gave public acknowledgement to the educational and social unease generated by the two-tier system operating via O level and CSE and amalgamated the two in 1986, with the first candidates being examined in 1988. The method of awarding grades in this new examination was arrived at after a complex and tense series of negotiations between the old O level boards and the CSE boards, culminating in the O level boards retaining the power to award marks at the A, B and C level, which corresponded to the old pass marks for O level, and the old CSE boards having jurisdiction over the rest of the grades D, E, F and G. Vested interest groups rarely relinquish their hold on status. The reason for pointing this out is that it remained fairly clear that in order to gain marks at that level, candidates either had to enter for the examined English Literature course, which naturally included Shakespeare, or they would do well to make sure some Shakespeare, or another representative of the pantheon of 'English Literary figures', featured in the coursework they were offering for moderation. The old divisions, in other words, had simply been reproduced under the umbrella of the new examination.

The kind of Shakespeare experience which pupils are offered is regulated by the GCSE rubrics for the set examination, and turns out to be a very similar experience to the earlier O level one: one which finds its persistent echo in all literature teaching from Quiller-Couch[7] to the National Curriculum. Some critics and commentators would argue that this is hardly surprising: that while literature has been harnessed in the service of the ideology of the capitalist state, for which it operates as a means of subjectifying the reader, emphasizing individualism at the expense of the social, and the universal at the expense of the historical, this kind of treatment is inevitable. According to this critical stance, from which not only is all recent post-structuralist theory excluded, but even such individually-located theories as reader response, the writer and the writer's writing are only capable of being analysed and 'appreciated' in terms of themselves and their 'effect'. Those critics whose theories do not fundamentally challenge the cultural dominance of the establishment are regularly cited, and feature on reading lists for students. Indeed, this critical reading will largely be what teachers are familiar with from their own sixth-form and college experience, and any alternative readings offered by post-modernists of any description will be mostly unknown. In this respect it is instructive to consider the influence of critics like Leavis, whose mark on the teaching of literature may be a little faded but largely remains indelible. Liberal humanism is clearly not the radical challenge it might once have appeared to be: its essential position, based on an unshakeable belief in the moral rightness of its practices, and for

Leavis as an individual on the importance of Englishness and a sense of national identity, can be seen now to have eventually chimed in with the cultural and social developments of the period from the first appearance of *Scrutiny* in 1932 to today. As Terry Eagleton points out: 'Whatever the failure or success of *Scrutiny* ... the fact remains that English students in England today are "Leavisites" whether they know it or not, irremediably altered by that historic intervention.'[8] This explains why even in 1990, in a syllabus for GCSE 1992, the Assessment Objectives include the ability by the candidate to: 'communicate a sensitive and informed personal response to what is read' (Midlands Examining Group). The Leavisite notion that literature makes you a better person still echoes among the examination syllabuses and statements of attainment.

Given this process of the gradual prising away from the English department stockroom walls of the fingers of the Bard and his disappearance into the brickwork, and the tacit recognition of the *de facto* position in schools apparent in GCSE examination syllabuses, what explains the inclusion of Shakespeare in the National Curriculum? Was there a parallel but different process going on which only surfaced officially with the publication of the Cox Report in 1989? To answer this question we need to look at the series of government-initiated reports which have served to operate as indicators of official thinking on the teaching of English, since the 1960s.

The parallel process was linked to and partly responsible for the kinds of examination demands described above. The exercises which hold English up for inspection and result in recommendations for action, were, and are, part of the evolving efforts to find a solution to the 'problem'. The problem in question is, of course, the proficiency or lack of it which contemporary school leavers are deemed to show in English, both written and spoken, and the ongoing diatribes about the state system which this provokes from employers. English provides the focal point for many of the culture's anxieties about itself, and the reiterated desire to re-establish the perceived situation of the past, naively believed to have been a time of 'certainties' and a totally literate and acquiescent population, is evidence of a disturbed and directionless society. The persistent attacks on English teaching which have characterized the period since the 1960s, particularly noticeable in the right-wing press, added to the already profound uncertainties within the teaching profession. And yet, when the first of these reports, the Bullock Report, was published in 1975, it could point back fifty years to the Newbolt Report of 1921 and quote exactly the same kinds of criticism from employers then: 'great difficulty in obtaining junior clerks who can speak and write English clearly and correctly'; 'our young employees are hopelessly deficient in their command of English'; 'teaching of English in the present day schools produces a very limited command of the English language'. The Bullock Report, while acknowledging that some of its own evidence produced similar observations, nevertheless addressed itself in a spirit of serious inquiry and professionalism to its task, which was to 'inquire into the teaching in the schools of reading and other uses of English'. In significant respects the

Report has never achieved the fundamental changes it recommended, and has never been absorbed into the pedagogical consciousness of more than a relative handful of teachers. As it was concerned initially with reading, what it has to say about literature is of some interest here. The Report refers back to earlier critics and writers in its attempt to evaluate the claims made for literature, and is honest enough to include those who do not take the consensus, Leavisite, view: 'In recent years it has been questioned whether literature does in fact make the reader a better and more sensitive human being'; and 'One American educationist (anonymous) has said bluntly that when it comes down to it there is no evidence that the reading of literature in schools produces in any way the social or emotional effects claimed for it.'[9]

There is no doubt that the Report itself does take the view that literature is a valuable experience, however it is 'done' in the classroom. What is revealed about the assumptions of the Committee of Inquiry is instructive. No overt reference to Leavis is made, but much use is made of his vocabulary – 'genuineness of response', 'no attention at all was given to the words on the page' (this a comment made in sorrow), 'true discernment' – otherwise, the references to critics and commentators, C.S. Lewis, Cecil Day Lewis, George Sampson, Nowell Smith, indicate an adherence to the status quo, the 1970s version of liberal humanism. Shakespeare is not mentioned in the Report, but can be dimly discerned in statements such as:

> There is an equal polarity of view on what should be done with literature in the classroom. To some teachers there is no question but that this should consist of a close and detailed examination of the text, each successive encounter an attempt to sharpen discrimination . . . [this] approach is traditionally thought appropriate for pupils preparing for examinations and, by extension, for pupils whose road will in due course lead there.

'Close and detailed examination of the text' reinforces conclusions to be reached from the expectations of examination syllabuses: Bullock does not question this method of experiencing a text, and is secure in knowing that this is a practice continued by consensus.

The Committee of Inquiry under the chairmanship of Sir Alan Bullock in 1972 was set up by Margaret Thatcher, then Secretary of State for Education. In 1979, when she became Prime Minister, it became clear that her views had at least some bearing on the judgement that the Bullock Report had not quite come up to scratch: that it had failed to offer the kind of 'grammar'-orientated view of English teaching favoured by many adherents of the Conservative Party. From this time on, starting in 1984, there has been a continuous production of reports and documents addressing the subject of English in schools. English is clearly at the root of the struggle being carried out in the education sector for ideological supremacy, control of the curriculum and of ideas and attitudes by the so-called radical right, and only with the production of the National Curriculum and its implementation has there been any indication that the 'what' has given way to the 'how'. The Bullock Report was followed by *English from 5 to 16: Curriculum Matters 1*, published in 1984, which put Shakespeare on the agenda for the first time by including in the Reading section of Objectives for 16-year-old pupils the following:

> Have some awareness of the relevance of imaginative literature to human experience; recognise some of the ways in which writers of fiction, poetry and plays achieve their effects; and have some ability to judge the value and quality of what they read;
> Have experienced some literature and drama of high quality, not limited to the twentieth century, including Shakespeare.[10]

The person responsible for the publication of *Curriculum Matters 1*, Jack Dalgleish, was HMI Staff Inspector for English, and had been a student of F.R. Leavis at Downing College, Cambridge. Here again are the hallmarks of the 'traditional' approach, and singled out for special attention is the notion of 'how writers achieve their effects'. The emphasis on literature of 'high quality', and the deliberate inclusion of pre-twentieth-century literature lays down a marker for the future National Curriculum. This is clearly going to be about, among other things, a recovery of some of the 'quality' that has been lost since the permissive 1960s, a requirement to recapture the values of the past.

Curriculum Matters 1 was followed by *Responses to Curriculum Matters 1*, in 1986,[11] containing a digest of responses to the original document which had been received from teachers and educationists. The wording of the reading objectives has been significantly altered: most 16-year-old students should have been offered a substantial experience of 'pleasurable and sustained encounters with a wide selection of fiction, poetry and drama (not confined to the twentieth century)'. Shakespeare has been omitted, reflecting with greater accuracy than the first document the actualities of the classroom, but the change in wording is also of interest: 'offered', 'pleasurable' and 'sustained encounters' refocus this activity on the pupil, and take account of the pupil's right to reject, unlike the original which seeks to impose a view of literature which suits the prevailing ethos. Quite apart from any questions of aesthetics or 'value', the original document assumes agreement about what is regarded as 'high-quality' imaginative literature. This indicates a certainty about the thinking and critical judgements of teachers in schools which begs some questions: if it can be presumed that teachers know what this literature is, and if, as is obvious, they know it to be 'high-quality' then why do they need to be *required* to teach it? Have they already abandoned it in favour of other literatures? If so, does this not indicate something about the nature of the pupils they are engaged in teaching that might make one wary of imposing traditional literature on them?

Whatever answers one might want to supply to these questions, they were not part of the agenda in the next report on English, the Report of the Committee of Inquiry into the Teaching of English Language, chaired by Sir John Kingman and published in March 1988. This committee of inquiry, set up while the

Education Reform Bill (to become the Education Reform Act of 1988) was before Parliament, had the brief 'to recommend a model of the English Language as a basis for teacher training and professional discussion, and to consider how far and in what ways that model should be made explicit to pupils at various stages of education'. Kingman is relevant to this discussion only in so far as the report finds itself unable to avoid some mention of literature: language in its literary forms (*pace* the view of language as capable of fragmentation into discrete kinds) is obviously part of a general inquiry into language. The Kingman Report (the members of the Kingman Committee included Professor Brian Cox) linked this idea of language to aesthetic development, and made two particular statements which were echoed in the later Cox Report:

> It is equally important for them [children] to read and hear and speak the great literature of the past. Our modern language and our modern writing have grown out of the language and literature of the past . . . We do not completely know what modern writing is unless we know what lies behind it.

and:

> It is possible that a generation of children may grow up deprived of their entitlement – an introduction to the powerful and splendid history of the best that has been thought and said in our language.

The lack of attribution for Matthew Arnold's description here can be passed over, but it is pertinent to link Arnold with the next sentence in this paragraph; where Arnold was defining culture and literature, so the Kingman report also acknowledges the centrality of culture:

> Too rigid a concern with what is 'relevant' to the lives of young people seems to us to pose the danger of impoverishing not only the young people, but the culture itself, which has to be revitalised by each generation.[12]

Before we move into an examination of the National Curriculum for English itself, and its preceding report, the Cox Report, some conclusions would be useful. The cumulative thrust of these reports and recommendations with regard to literature, and particularly with regard to Shakespeare, is to outline a desirable position which in all respects is backward-looking, generated by a desire to recapture, to recuperate a threatened certainty. Concern is implicit in these documents that not only has 'great' literature been moved from centre stage, but that it might be pushed right off into the wings. The position to which they would all like to return is the safe haven where literature is used to reaffirm cultural and ideological stances palatable to the writers, and where the statements in which they have expressed their affiliations are accepted as self-evident truths.

The Cox Report of June 1989 set the final seal on all these earlier recommendations by including in its Reading Attainment Target stipulations that pupils aiming at level 7 and upwards (recognizable as pupils in the GCSE examination age group) should 'read a range of poetry, fiction, literary non-fiction and drama, including works written before the twentieth century', and in the Programmes of Study for reading recommends that pupils should 'gain some experience of the works of Shakespeare'. In many other respects Cox's antecedents in Kingman and before can also be traced, even down to the particular phrasing of some statements. But this report very clearly singles out Shakespeare, and gives him individual emphasis and status beyond what was accorded him in any previous document. The ways in which this inclusion of Shakespeare were achieved are the subject of the next chapter. The reasons for this inclusion, which are the subject of the rest of this chapter, are equally illuminating.

In addition to the obvious build-up of pressure and intent from these earlier documents, two individuals share the responsibility for the inclusion of Shakespeare in the National Curriculum: Professor Brian Cox, the chairman of the English Working Group and Dr Rex Gibson, progenitor of the 'Shakespeare in Schools' project which was still in active operation when Dr Gibson gave evidence to the Working Group.[13]

Professor Cox and Dr Gibson represent two versions of what is essentially the same view of Shakespeare: that he is 'great', and that pupils should have experience of this greatness in schools. Whereas Professor Cox is confined by his own area of expertise into describing Shakespeare and his own adherence to him in a relatively theoretical, conceptual way, Dr Gibson underpins his views with a passionate exposition of practical ways in which pupils can be given experience of Shakespeare. Professor Cox, speaking at a meeting of English teachers, not only revealed the way in which he became chairman of the English Working Group (all other invitees having declined the offer, he was personally invited by the then Secretary of State, Mr Kenneth Baker, to become chairman; an interesting indication of the way the task was regarded by the anonymous other possible chairpersons), but also described the ways in which Dr Gibson convinced the Working Group of the absolute rightness of including Shakespeare in the National Curriculum. This he did, among other things, by getting all the committee members on their feet to insult each other in the language of Caliban and Prospero, the sheer unfamiliarity of which highly energetic exercise clearly had the desired effect.

Professor Cox, in a personal interview, further elaborated on his reasons for wanting Shakespeare in the National Curriculum, and makes clear that his views express the belief in the 'cultural heritage' Shakespeare who is the birthright of all pupils. Professor Cox's views are not surprising: what makes them interesting is their closeness to establishment valuations of Shakespeare which have been current for the last 150 years – in short, there has been no development from this point of view, no acknowledgement of other factors which may make a revaluation timely. Professor Cox has four main reasons for wanting Shakespeare in the National Curriculum: first, the belief that the kind of 'great' literature written by Shakespeare encompasses wisdom; second, that 'these great works' are part of our cultural heritage, are central to our culture, and that every child has the right to be introduced to them; third, that Shakespeare 'uses language in a way beyond that of any other writer, and his language has been influential beyond that of any other writer.' Lastly, that Shakespeare has greater insight into human character than other writers. Additional reasons are that the history of the development of the English language is intimately bound up with Shakespeare's language, and that to deprive pupils of the experience of this language, and this knowledge, is as bad and diminishing as depriving pupils of the opportunity to become competent in Standard English.

A plethora of questions is provoked by these views: Whose culture? What wisdom? Who defined it as wisdom? In what ways are these works central to our culture? What does Professor Cox mean by cultural heritage – the heritage of which people? How has this language of Shakespeare been influential? The juxtaposition of notions of 'cultural heritage', 'birthright','greatness' and Standard English imply their own ideological provenance and, at a time of anxieties about standards, ideas of national identity and access to a universally understood version of English, indicate a paternalist, establishment perspective on contemporary challenges. However, Professor Cox enlarged on these views later in the interview, making clear that while he sounds like a traditionalist, and one might expect such a traditionalist to have a corresponding attitude to the teaching of Shakespeare, he actually holds quite opposite views when it comes to the classroom experience of Shakespeare; for example, he regards the whole idea of teaching Shakespeare so that pupils can write 'lit. crit.' essays as 'stupid'. This pupil-centred approach does represent a shift into a revaluation of how to teach Shakespeare – but Professor Cox's whole approach to the teaching of English is characterized by such enlightened views; he feels, for example, that the experiential, active engagement with Shakespeare is what matters, and regards what he calls the 'English habit' of keeping pupils quiet in class as incomprehensible, and asks what purpose it is supposed to serve. He regards passivity and repression as the outcomes of an outdated and negative curriculum, which by implication does nothing to enhance pupils' sense of self, either in social or cultural terms.[14]

Professor Cox presents something of a paradox, which is, I think, not unusual in the education world, and is quite understandable as a version of 'British compromise'. While holding unshakeable convictions about the place and importance of 'great' literature (feeling, for example, that a curriculum which does not include great writers deprives pupils of their cultural birthright) and still holding a view of literature as something which 'embodies and promulgates attitudes and moral values', and obviously not having found anything, either in new critical positions or political challenge, to make him alter these constructions of literature and culture, nevertheless Professor Cox does take a challenging – and for many teachers, therefore, a threatening – approach to classroom practice. Will Professor Cox's Shakespeare remain the same after he has been experienced in these ways in the classroom?

Dr Gibson represents a different paradox. He, too, is utterly convinced of the importance of Shakespeare, but much less for any reasons to do with cultural worth, and much more to do with what the experience of Shakespeare, undertaken in an active participatory way, makes possible in the classroom for pupils of all ages and all abilities. Dr Gibson's commitment is to the exploration, by whatever means, of the enormous possibilities of Shakespeare's language. The 'Shakespeare in Schools' project, admiringly described in the Cox Report, by operating as both a research and a teaching project, has been able to establish a very wide bank of ideas and practical suggestions for teaching Shakespeare in this way. The paradox is this: Dr Gibson is so convinced of the rightness of including Shakespeare in the National Curriculum, and so keen that pupils should experience Shakespeare, that he is prepared to contemplate the risk that most pupils' experience of Shakespeare will remain minimal, boring, text- and desk-bound, simply because most teachers have not had access to the kind of approach which he is supporting. The advocacy of Dr Gibson and Professor Cox, while clearly underpinned by the recent separate statements about Shakespeare in other documents already alluded to, and therefore not some idiosyncratic whim of their own, has been so successful that in the Schools Examination and Assessment Council's *English Criteria*, GCSE applicable to examinations in and from 1994, we find the following:

> This range [of printed material] should draw upon both contemporary and pre-twentieth century literature, including some of those works whose influence in shaping and refining the English language and its literature is recognised, most notably the works of Shakespeare.[15]

The same language, repeated from document to document, stipulates the same literature, and makes sure that no pupil aiming to do GCSE can succeed without some Shakespeare in the syllabus. There has been no challenge to this position, except from the unnamed members of the Working Group who did not agree – unanimous agreement about Shakespeare's inclusion in the National Curriculum was not reached, as the Report makes clear.[16] Disagreement is a dangerous affair when it is about Shakespeare and about entitlement – can anyone seriously *not* want pupils to experience some Shakespeare? What kind of cultural position are you taking if you do disagree? Recent responses from some teachers have been expressed as the fervent hope that it would all go away, and die a death, but as the GCSE document quoted above makes clear, this will not happen until at least after 1994.

3 English for ages 5 to 16

I propose to look in some detail in this chapter at the ways in which Shakespeare is referred to in the National Curriculum documents, and to suggest how teachers depending on these statements for any kind of advice and pointers in the right direction will find little to help them. The main references to Shakespeare occur in the Cox Report of 1989,[1] and while this document has largely been superseded by the Orders in Council of 1990, it remains the substantive document containing the theoretical and philosophical rationale for the kinds of English teaching and experience demanded in the National Curriculum for English.

The reference to Shakespeare in Chapter 16 of the Report is significantly different in several key aspects from the much longer reference in Chapter 7, which was not included in the final document in its entirety. I propose to discuss these two references in relation to each other, attempting to draw out their significance for teachers and pupils.

Chapter 16

The Chapter 16 reference, which is made in the Programmes of Study for Reading, is contained in the following statements:

16.31: In particular they [teachers] should give pupils the opportunity to gain some experience of the works of Shakespeare. Using sensitivity and tact, teachers should help pupils to tackle texts of increasing difficulty.

and:

16.40: Pupils working towards level 7 should read some texts written for adults, . . . including Shakespeare. They should discuss the themes, settings, characters and literary styles of the texts in order to make a personal response to them.

The reasons given in this chapter for including Shakespeare, and other pre-twentieth century writers, are that 'pupils should be introduced to some of the works which have been most influential in shaping and refining the English language and its literature'. These statements from Chapter 16 do say roughly what one would expect given the circumstances of their production. 'Sensitivity and tact' are easily recognized as the hallmarks of the good classroom practitioner; 'discussing the themes, settings, characters and literary style of the texts' is an activity with which we are all familiar, particularly if we teach A level English; 'to make a personal response' is, of course, what we want our pupils to do. And 'works which have been most influential in shaping and refining the English language and its literature' expresses in a vague, generalized kind of way how we feel the relationship between language and literature operates.

I would argue here, however, that there is a great deal in these apparently uncontentious statements which needs challenging. The given rationale for including these 'great' writers in the document (Dickens, Wordsworth and the Authorised Version of the Bible are also included) by no means confirms the foregone conclusion that works or writers have been influential in shaping, or refining the English language and its literature. At the very least this statement reveals a lack of acknowledgement of the extensive work done in the last half-century by linguists and theorists on the ways in which language changes and develops.[2] It also begs the question, very seriously, of which English language and which English literature we mean. This formulation runs significantly counter to statements made elsewhere in the National Curriculum document, which at least acknowledge notions of varieties of English language, and actively point out the existence of many literatures written in other Englishes. It would be interesting to be told a little more about this single-handed shaping and refining of the English language, and about how it is supposed to have occurred. There is another, unstated, rationale at work here, which connects at very deep levels with the whole political and social context operating at the time the English committee was deliberating. It is to do with reasserting some sense of cultural status, recovering cultural identity and power in the face of current challenges to the whole idea of 'English' and 'literature' being articulated by hitherto marginalized groups now seeking a political voice and cultural status of their own.[3]

One can perhaps see why those particular words were used to express this idea, but it is difficult to see what we are supposed to do with this notion in the classroom. Is this statement actually testable or verifiable? Can I take a work by a 'great' writer, say Wordsworth, and show how it helped 'shape' and 'refine' the language and literature that came after it? If I cannot, then what function does this statement serve? Is it, as I believe, simply an assertion included for other purposes, or can it serve any real purpose for teachers? It does appear to be an attempt to lock them into a particular role which corresponds with current ideological demands.

Far from acknowledging any more recent critical theory, the Cox Report simply refers to 'literature' and 'language' assuming that we all know what is meant, and that we all agree with its own constructions. There is a glossing over here of the whole process by which that which we agree to call 'literature' is produced, disseminated, and 'encultured'; instead, a readership is assumed which adheres to the conventional 'School of English' views of literature and language still largely taught at many universities and colleges of higher education, as well as, of course, in schools. Terry Eagleton puts it characteristically:

> Some texts are born literary, some achieve literariness, and some have literariness thrust upon them. Breeding in this respect may count for a good deal more then birth. What matters may not be where you came from but how people treat you. If they decide that you are literature then it seems that you are, irrespective of what you thought you were.[4]

when he argues that literature is no more fixed and definable as literature than any other writing, and that the value attached to that writing which we have agreed to call 'literature' is entirely a product of a set of social, ideological and cultural conditions, both past and present. In other words, Eagleton suggests that there are no immutable rules governing the allocation of the label 'literature' to any specific writings, and that what may be regarded highly in one age may be discarded by the next.

The statement at paragraph 16.31 of the Cox Report, embracing the notion of teachers using 'sensitivity and tact', indicates particular aspects of classroom interaction, including the relative social status of teacher and pupils, the 'hidden curriculum' as it forms part of this structure, and the teacher's own attitudes towards this literature, which are not opened up for investigation here or anywhere else in the document. Apart from anything else, how does this sensitivity manifest itself? And towards what, about what? Alan Sinfield suggests what is actually happening to pupils in this 'sensitive' context:

> the pupil is being persuaded to internalise success or failure with particular and relative cultural codes as an absolute judgement on her or his potential as a human being,[5]

particularly where the pupil

> is himself being judged each time he responds in class to a piece of literature. More is at stake than his knowledge of the text. Is the value-judgement he forms the one the teacher finds acceptable? Is he betraying himself, he may well ask, as one who lacks discrimination?[6]

This is apparently the kind of purpose of the 'sensitivity' referred to in the Cox Report, and along with the use of 'tact' it implies a certain ideological position for the teacher: one of cultural 'superiority' which depends on the teacher mediating the literature to the pupils and already knowing what response is required. The use of the word 'tackle' reveals a view of the literary text as a given, unchanging object, a view which much recent critical work is at pains to reappraise. The view of the teacher, the text and the pupil contained in this statement will inevitably bring in its wake precisely those kinds of difficulty which the aforementioned 'tact' will have to overcome. If, instead of the kind of sharing, exploratory model of learning which is implied in other parts of the Report, the experience of literature, and particularly of Shakespeare, is to be the one implied here, then large amounts of this sensitivity and tact will be vital. There is an underlying feeling here that the authors of the Report recognize that the literature they are talking about carries with it so much cultural and 'establishment' baggage that many pupils will resist it. Ironically, the very approaches opened up and made available by modern critical theory which could help to circumvent these resistances in favour of a different kind of engagement with the text, remain unmentioned in this document. The Kingman Report, the immediate predecessor to this Report, now largely ignored, does recognize these developments:

> The recent structuralist and post-structuralist revolutions in literary theory have caused people to think very energetically and critically about the relationship between the structures of language and the structure of thought, as well as the relationship between the structures of language and the structures of our culture.[7]

Some pointers in the general direction of some of this critical work would have been of great value within the Report.

Thirdly, located firmly in the same ideological position, we have the statement at paragraph 16.40 which seems to be trying to have its cake and eat it. Apart from the interesting implications of texts 'written for adults' in a paragraph about pupils of 14 years and upwards, two contradictory ideas have been set in conjunction, rather than in opposition to each other: 'They should discuss the themes, settings, characters and literary styles of the texts' in order to 'make a personal response to them'. When pupils in the classroom undertake this activity with their teacher they are in effect being inculcated into a way of responding to the texts which has been established over the years,[8] and by a school of criticism that owes nothing to the late twentieth century, as one which is suitable for A level literature study, and which depends on language being used and understood in predetermined and narrowly specific critical and cultural ways. Success in acquiring this skill marks out the pupil as worthy of higher things, and certainly as eligible for inclusion in certain elite groups. There is nothing personal in this process: it involves conventional forms of expression, set responses, an acceptable and taught set of lexical labels to denote processes and relationships within the texts in accordance with this particular ideological view, and above all regards the text as a fixed product. It 'means', and both the teacher's job and the pupil's task is to learn and communicate that 'meaning'. Once this process has been undergone, it is doubtful how much of a personal response is possible. A truly 'personal' response, one which rests on an engagement with a text untrammelled by 'lit. crit.' teaching, is, I suspect, only ever achieved in spite of this approach, and not because of it. The approach implied here is not interested in the pupils' experiences, in what they bring to bear on the texts, or in the personal, individual meaning that pupils may make with the text – only after the required initiation will they be invited to make a personal response.

In conclusion, Chapter 16 sets out the requirements to be made of teachers and pupils, and, as I have indicated, points back to the past in every respect with regard to critical position, classroom practice, examination work and ways of engaging with the texts.

Chapter 7

Paragraph 7.16 of the Cox Report contains the rationale behind the inclusion of Shakespeare, which falls into two main parts: one dealing with theories about Shakespeare and his position in our culture; the other describing the practical means, demonstrated by the 'Shakespeare in Schools' project, for making Shakespeare available to all pupils.

The first part of paragraph 7.16 runs as follows:

> 7.16: Many teachers believe that Shakespeare's work conveys universal values, and that his language expresses rich and subtle meanings beyond that of any other English writer. Other teachers point out that evaluations of Shakespeare have varied from one historical period to the next, and they argue that pupils should be encouraged to think critically about his status in the canon. But almost everyone agrees that his work should be represented in a National Curriculum. Shakespeare's plays are so rich that in every age they can produce fresh meanings, and even those who deny his universality agree on his cultural importance.

Apart from the intriguing spectacle opened up for the imagination by the 'many teachers' and the 'other teachers' disagreeing about which valuation to place on Shakespeare, and the very helpful 'almost everyone' who thinks he should be in the National Curriculum, the actual statements made here about Shakespeare are of most concern for this examination. The statements fall into three categories: those which make assertions about Shakespeare; those which acknowledge dissent from these views; and one which proposes a classroom approach. To clarify this, let us list the *assertions* together:

● Shakespeare's work conveys universal values;
● his language expresses rich and subtle meanings beyond that of any other English writer;
● Shakespeare's plays are so rich that in every age they can produce fresh meanings.

These statements are of the generalized kind that readily gain our agreement on a casual first reading of the document: given that most readers of the document will have gone through an English literature experience that told them those things, this is hardly surprising. But there are alternative constructions to be put on these assertions, which would see them as producing a decontextualized, dehistoricized Shakespeare, whose language appeared ready-made, plucked out of nowhere; the kind of Shakespeare who occupies that value-free literary limbo inhabited by those who have been clever enough to produce 'the best that has been thought and said', *pace* Matthew Arnold, and whose readers are buoyed up into ethereal regions by the richness of the language which they can endlessly unravel in their pursuit of the meaning of these subtleties.

The phrase 'universal values' is itself highly culturally charged, and is used here as a way of emphasizing a view of Shakespeare which it suits current ideology to take, and which aids a process of mystification. It is worth quoting Terry Eagleton again here:

> Since literature, as we know, deals in universal human values rather than in such historical trivia as civil wars, the oppression of women, or the dispossession of the English peasantry, it could serve to place in cosmic perspective the petty demands of working people for decent living conditions or greater control over their own lives, and might even with luck come to render them oblivious of such issues in their high-minded contemplation of eternal truths and beauties.[9]

In spite of the people who 'deny his universality' the National Curriculum statement nevertheless manages to convey that 'Shakespeare conveys universal values'. The ironical tone of Eagleton's statement serves to point up just how enmeshed it is possible to be in lofty contemplation of Shakespeare, and how powerfully this ideology works. However, we might ask, what exactly are we being asked to engage with when we contemplate universal values? The best answer I can think of, in terms of the National Curriculum document, is an A level mode critical engagement, which includes precisely those features of the text isolated in the recommendations in paragraph 16.40, with some reference to 'rich and subtle meanings', all of which serves to give us a panoramic and all-embracing view of the universe. But, if we are also engaged in disinterring from their current burial in the works 'civil war, oppression of women, and the dispossession of the English peasantry', I suspect 'universal values' would require a speedy reappraisal.

By way of an example, the conventional ideology would come up with the following about *The Merchant of Venice*: 'This concord has been hard-won in "The Merchant of Venice" but it is achieved with a gracious dignity and with wit'.[10] This is the final sentence in an introduction which simply ignores much of what is in the play. A reading which showed how money, racism and the treatment of women operated in the text would be hard put to it to use words like 'concord', 'gracious dignity' or 'wit' with any degree of sincerity, but these seem to be the kinds of words which signal 'universal values'. However, to pursue a search for these values, it is worth asking where they are – in the events of the play, or in individual lines? When lines like 'The quality of mercy is not strained' are quoted *hors de texte*, is this because of their supposed universality, or is it not rather that by decontextualizing them a spurious kind of 'truth' appears to be expressed by them which comes in handy on all sorts of occasions?

It is not very difficult to demolish the whole edifice of the notion of 'universal values' with regard to each play in turn, but the cultural pedestal occupied by Shakespeare is far more difficult to dismantle, and, unfortunately for teachers, 'universal values' is one of the materials of which it is made.

The Merchant of Venice provides a useful context in which to examine further the uses to which 'universal values' can be, and are, put. In the name of achieving a serene overview which stresses 'concord' and 'dignity', the New Penguin editor does some revealing things in his Introduction. For example, although six of the first 14 scenes of the play are located in Belmont, and would seem to indicate that the text is giving a roughly equal weighting to Portia/Belmont and Shylock/Antonio/Venice, the editor can only come up with this statement about the casket test:

> Portia's father may have denied some of our concerns for a lover's freedom of choice in his beloved ... but the coherence of the play, the movement of the dramatic poetry, take us beyond these doubts and cavillings. We are convinced of the essential sanity of the casket test for Portia's suitors.[11]

and offers one additional statement:

> [Portia] is in fact nicely poised between a proper subservience to her father's will and a caustic rejection of all the suitors.[12]

Apart from the innately anti-feminist stance here, the editor does not begin to question several aspects of the play which might challenge his kind of reading. He simply ignores them. Elements which are uncomfortable, like the power of fathers to make such provision and conditions for their daughters, the significance of each suitor, the framing this sets up for the significance of Bassanio's suit, and the location of all this in a text pervaded by concern with money, are not addressed by this editor. This construction of the play by this editor fits very snugly into the 'universal values' bracket, indeed exemplifies it, but also disables a more complex and questioning reading of the play. It is this process of making everything safe for bourgeois sensibilities which is what 'universal values' is about, and why it is so debilitating.

> Almost invariably it is assumed that the plays reveal universal 'human' values and qualities and that they are self-contained and coherent entities; and the activity of criticism in producing these assumptions is effaced.[13]

Precisely.

The second of the three assertions, that 'his language expresses rich and subtle meanings beyond that of any other English writer' indicates the same provenance as the first one, that is, an ideological construction which severs Shakespeare from his own historical and cultural context, and which also disregards what we know about language and the making of meaning. Quite apart from any pertinent linguistic theories, this statement is so generalized and unverifiable, particularly in the classroom context, that it simply further develops the mystifying process.

A critical process which could provide the kind of enabling stance closed off by the language of the Report is that of semiotics, and in the following quotation from Alessandro Serpieri the immense complexities of meaning made possible in Shakespeare's texts are acknowledged in language well beyond the simplification of 'rich and subtle':

> The literary sign is powerfully overdetermined, that is to say, it gathers sense through a wide network of syntactic and semantic relations manifest in the text itself by its very textual situation – a situation that endows it at once with syntagmatic (horizontal) and paradigmatic (vertical) meanings – over and above those values that it assumes through its macrotextual allegiances (the rapport the single text entertains with other works within the Shakespearean canon) and intertextual allegiances (the relationship of the text with other texts in general). But it likewise, and no less crucially, takes on meaning from the historical, cultural and pragmatic contexts within which it is produced. The literary sign, in other words, brings together a complex of meanings at the crossroads between the different routes of signification: textual, extratextual, linguistic and semiotic.

Serpieri acknowledges the complex density of Shakespeare:

> Shakespearean dramaturgy remains one of the most stimulating texts for semioticians of drama, both for the theoretical returns it offers regarding dramatic operations, at the highest possible level of complexity and of semiotic polyvalency, and for the critical-interpretative paths it opens to a coherent, but at the same time problematic, textual exploration.[14]

I am not suggesting here that all teachers should take to semiotics, but that a gesture in the direction of these possibilities in the Report would have been welcome, and that the very language of these allusions to Shakespeare in the Report acts powerfully in the opposite direction.

The third of the three assertions, that 'Shakespeare's plays are so rich that in every age they can produce fresh meanings' is of the same order as the other two, and merely limply indicates a recognition of changes of interpretation over the years. It would be very surprising if Shakespeare, or indeed any other writer for that matter, did not produce fresh meanings in every age, although it is not quite clear how this squares with 'universal values'.

> 'Our' Shakespeare is not identical with that of his contemporaries; it is rather that different historical periods have constructed a 'different' . . . Shakespeare for their own purposes and found in these texts elements to value or devalue, though not necessarily. All literary works, in other words, are 're-written', if only unconsciously, by the societies which read them; indeed there is no reading of a work which is not also a 're-writing'.[15]

It is clearly not just Shakespeare whose words produce fresh meanings in every age, so whatever quality of Shakespeare the writers of the Report were attempting to define still remains elusive. The reference to Shakespeare's plays being 'so rich', although we are not told in what, ties this assertion firmly to the other two and makes clear, again, that all three assertions have been made for ideological rather than pedagogical reasons, where the kind of Shakespeare being constructed and offered to the readers of the National Curriculum document is one which the authors can assume we will all recognize.

The second group of statements from the first part of paragraph 7.16, those indicating *dissent*, are the following:

- almost everyone agrees that his work should be represented in the National Curriculum;
- even those who deny his universality agree on his cultural importance.

The first of these two statements provides an interesting indication of the lack of complete agreement within the English Working Group. The second can also be regarded as belonging more properly to an analysis of why Shakespeare has been included in the National Curriculum for English, but it does also include the very significant allusion to the perceived cultural importance of Shakespeare, as agreed on by people who deny his universality. This acknowledgement of other critical viewpoints which deny the universality of Shakespeare opens up for inspection alternative evaluations, and, by indicating their existence, invites this inspection. However, 'cultural importance' is not opened up for any kind of discussion because everyone agrees that it is so.

The foregoing discussion of the other statements both in Chapter 16 and Chapter 7 on Shakespeare in the National Curriculum will have indicated already some of the constructions that can be made of 'cultural importance'. Raymond Williams proposed three definitions of 'culture': first, a general process of intellectual, spiritual and aesthetic development; second, a particular way of life, whether of a people, a period or a group, or humanity in general; and third, the works and practices of intellectual and especially artistic activity.[16] It would be possible to fit Shakespeare into each of these definitions, and to fit each of these definitions into what we think we are doing with Shakespeare in the classroom, but it is not clear which of the three most closely coincides with what the Report writers had in mind. In terms of the general permeation of our social and political lives by the Shakespeare myth, which includes a vast range of constructs, performances, quotations, advertising, the old Bank of England £20 note, commodities, book titles, tourism, 'heritage', and so on, it is clear that Shakespeare is of cultural importance. What is not obvious is quite how this weight of significance is to be brought to bear on work in the classroom, and which particular aspect of it the writers would like us to be examining. In other words, what do we *do* with Shakespeare in the classroom to make the experience for pupils at all commensurate with this cultural load?

There is a very powerful ideological position in relation to this, expressed by Malcolm Evans:

> For all these children [involved in Shakespeare Commemoration Day celebrations in 1922] there would be no escape from the work of Shakespeare, presented here not as a set of historical documents in a language already to a marked extent 'foreign' but as an essential and supreme element of the 'Great Mother-Tongue', which will condemn those who do not master it to a kind of exile within their own language.[17]

This view was also expressed by Professor Brian Cox, Chairman of the English Working Party, when he said in personal discussion that to know nothing of Shakespeare is to be 'sidelined', and that 'Shakespeare is a point of reference and embodies our cultural heritage'.

The Malcolm Evans irony is clear, while the sincerity of Professor Cox's position exemplifies the collective voice of a predominately white, male, middle-class England, which for good liberal reasons seeks to share some of the cultural largess to be enjoyed through experience of the works of Shakespeare. This conflation of Shakespeare with English and Englishness is not made open for inspection by teachers and pupils. What the National Curriculum is requiring teachers to do is to deliver up the works via the current conventional treatment to the pupils in their classrooms.

This position might appear to be immediately undermined by the second part of paragraph 7.16:

> The 'Shakespeare in Schools' project, at the Cambridge Institute of Education, has shown that secondary pupils of a wide range of abilities can find Shakespeare accessible, meaningful and enjoyable. The project has demonstrated that the once-traditional method where desk-bound pupils read the text has been advantageously replaced by exciting, enjoyable approaches that are social, imaginative and physical. This can also be achieved by: use of film and video recordings, visits to live theatre performances, participation in songs and dances, dramatic improvisations, activities in which Shakespeare's language is used by pupils interacting with each other. Pupils exposed to this type of participatory, exploratory approach to literature can acquire a firm foundation to proceed to more formal literary responses should they subsequently choose to do so.

A close examination reveals exactly the same ideological position underpinning what looks like a 'Shakespeare at any cost' range of practices, and arriving inexorably at the end back at our old friend 'lit. crit.'

Nevertheless, there are some indications here of useful practical approaches, although considerations of space prevent any detailed discussion of possibilities. Some of the notions expressed here do need challenging, however. The first is that reading Shakespeare in class by desk-bound pupils is 'once-traditional', whereas unfortunately it is still the experience of many pupils who do Shakespeare at all, and the second is the very revealing connection made between these newer approaches and the 'firm foundation' they are seen to make possible, and the 'more formal literary responses' which they will enable at a later date. The framework within which the whole experience is perceived is shown here to be closed in by conventional procedures of literary appreciation and study about which no discussion is allowed.

The use of film and video recordings, while already a well-established practice in many schools for the purposes of familiarizing pupils with the story and maybe some of the language of Shakespeare's plays, is a practice that in my view needs challenging quite fundamentally. Its inclusion here as a suggestion makes it quite likely that it will be the main, and possibly the only, experience of Shakespeare which many pupils will have in schools, particularly where teachers have not had access to any further training or classroom support.

The Shakespeare statements in the National Curriculum Report undoubtedly do raise all the questions asked here, and possibly many others, but at the same time the requirement to enable pupils to experience Shakespeare is to be welcomed for reasons which run counter to the ideological orientation of the Report. Ways of realizing these opposing views and of removing Shakespeare from the straitjacket of conventional studies are the subject of Part Three of this book.

4 Teachers and Shakespeare

In this chapter I want to look at the kinds of experience of Shakespeare which teachers will have had before becoming teachers, both as sixth-formers and as further education students; what A level and further education courses still offer by way of experience of Shakespeare, and what they demand of students; and how currently practising teachers regard their new obligation under the National Curriculum for English to teach Shakespeare to all pupils aiming for Keystage 4, or GCSE qualification. This kind of overview is of key importance in assessing the challenge to teachers of this obligation, and, as I shall show, their previous experiences of Shakespeare ensure that the task will be extremely difficult.

In the preceding chapters I have shown how Shakespeare has been constructed as the national cultural icon, and that that position not only confers on the works of Shakespeare certain cultural and literary values and attitudes, but also enables experience of those texts to be used to inculcate similar values and attitudes into each new generation of students. While this function of the texts remains largely implicit and unarticulated, it can nevertheless be traced in and recuperated from many current A level assessment objectives and essay questions.

For example, for the academic year 1989–1990, the examination boards which I shall be using as examples (Joint Matriculation Board, Associated Examining Board, Oxford Delegacy of Local Examinations, Cambridge Local Examinations Syndicate and the London Board[1] all prescribed assessment objectives that would have been instantly recognizable to a teacher of 50 years ago or more. In other words, these objectives are what one might call 'traditional'. The author, Shakespeare, is assumed to be in 'authority' over his texts, which display his intentionality and purpose, and which yield up proof of his aim to those who study him in the approved manner; Shakespeare as writer is taken to have conscious and deliberate control over all that the text 'says'. Students will be expected to 'recognise, appreciate and comment' on the ways in which writers (Shakespeare) handle(s) language, structure and content. All these boards are concerned that students comment on the 'use of language' in the texts: the phrasing of this requirement presupposes an experience of the texts which will convey them as fixed and deliberate. Other aspects of the texts to be looked at, such as the 'values expressed' in them, and the 'literary topics' taken to reside in them, imply a view of language as transparent, referring to and expressing values and congregations of ideas which are assumed to inhere in the words in which they are written. The currently available critical and interpretative approaches which build on and develop the work of such linguists as Ferdinand de Saussure, Lacan, Derrida and Barthes, and which offer radical alternatives to the understanding of language and 'use of language', have so far not permeated the thinking of A level examiners.[2] The text is clearly regarded by the boards as a 'given', and the features of the texts which students are to be rendered competent in decoding are recognizably the same as those singled out by critics in the early years of this century.

Students are in fact expected to show an interestingly difficult collection of responses: personal, imaginative, enjoyment and appreciation, but – and this is an important but – none of the responses is allowed to be free and unconstrained: personal response must be 'intelligent and sensitive' (AEB); enjoyment and appreciation must be recorded in a disciplined and critical way (AEB); not only is personal response looked for, but understanding of the 'causes of that response' will be expected (JMB); independent opinions and 'informed' judgements are asked for in addition to something called an 'imaginative response' (Oxford). The contradictions implied by these opposing demands are clear, and are echoed in Cox Report adumbrations about the teaching of literature. Students who wish to be admitted to the elect will have to show that they are intelligent, sensitive, imaginative, capable of personal response, independent, informed – one of the astonishing aspects of this is that by some process of collective but tacit agreement most teachers embarking on A level teaching will have a fairly clear idea of what all this means, or rather what A level examiners mean by it. The shared presuppositions upon which this whole edifice is built are testimony to the tenacity of classic realism as a critical practice, and the powerful way in which it has pervaded most literary and critical thinking since the late nineteenth century. But we must be clear about this. What is wanted is independence and personal response, but only so far. Nothing which cannot also be characterized as intelligent, informed and sensitive will do. The influence of Leavis is also evident here. Each of these yardsticks is, of course, itself highly culturally signified, belonging to an approach intended to produce a particular kind of liberal/humanist student whose interaction with the texts will be contained within the limits set by these signifiers.

When we turn to the A level essay questions which set out the contexts within which these responses are to be expressed, we can see in greater detail the kinds of interaction which they demand from teachers and students. Not surprisingly, questions from past papers are analysed year by year by teachers involved in this exercise for clues they give about the particular preoccupations and slant of each board, so a self-perpetuating circle of response and demand is maintained. A question like ' "Hamlet's tragic situation is heightened by the failure of other characters to understand him". Discuss' (JMB, 1984) indicates the following assumptions: Hamlet is clearly taken to be a *person*, who is in a tragic situation (left to the student to define). The phrasing of this pre-empts inspection of this double assumption because the real question at the heart of this statement is located further on, in the words 'heightened' and 'failure'. Hamlet is now revealed as a 'character', who is surrounded by other 'characters' who fail to understand him – *who* is it they fail to understand? *What* they fail to understand might be more helpful here. No mention is made of the fact that this is a *play*, and questions like this construct the text as a fixed entity containing or referring to fixed characters who are constructed as real people who, like Hamlet the 'real' person, have failures. No possibilities are opened up which would allow students to step outside the world of the text to look at it as an artefact, as a construction itself. While any student who attempted to discuss the contradictions and ambiguities furnished by the text might very well be given due credit for it, the very language in which the question is couched makes such a risky attempt highly unlikely.

A question like 'Discuss Shakespeare's use of real and assumed madness in *Hamlet*' (Cambridge, 1965) appears to be inviting the student to attempt an evaluation of Shakespeare's ability as a playwright, and the efficacy or otherwise of his 'use' of madness in the play, and insists that there is both real and assumed madness in the play without inviting any challenge to that idea. Attention is focused on the author as controller of the text and all its meanings, and looks like an attempt to insert assessment of authorial voice into a context which quite patently does not have one. Again, the fact of *Hamlet* as a play is ignored.

There are, nevertheless, questions which look as though they might allow another approach: ' "Corruption at Elsinore is all-pervading: no one escapes contamination." Discuss' (JMB, 1985), offers possibilities of interrogation which will focus on specific meanings of the language of the play, and a discussion of the meaning of the word 'corruption', but there are still two obstacles in the way of any radically alternative approach. Elsinore is given as an actual place, not even referred to here as the name of the 'place' in the play (quite patently we never *see* Elsinore on the stage, unless we happen to be there as in Laurence Olivier's renowned production of 1937[3] and even then the Elsinore building is not the one that existed either in Shakespeare's time, or in the time of Saxo Grammaticus[4]) which we must assume is what the *reader* of the text will imagine, 'in the mind's eye'. It is, with the word 'Denmark', the only referrant for the 'place' where these dramatic (in the sense of 'on a stage') events occur. In addition, no distinction is made between the indoor closed world of the palace, and other outside places indicated by the text: is the gravedigger implicated in this corruption? is Fortinbras? are the players? Secondly, the invitation is to discuss this corruption simply in terms of itself. In relation to what ideals, or moral values, is this corruption being posited? Students are therefore denied any historical context within which to discuss this corruption, are not specifically invited to discuss corruption as a corollary to power-holding and power-seeking, and are not invited to investigate any culturally defined meanings for these two words which would render such a discussion conscious of its own cultural place.

A question which appears to offer some departure from the classic realist norm of approach is the following: 'By isolating the character of Hamlet from the dramatic context we form a false impression of the whole play. Discuss' (Cambridge, 1965). Here, there is at least some acknowledgement that this text is a play, and forces attention onto Hamlet as a *character* rather than implying that he is a person. The question does offer opportunities to the student to show that she understands the wholeness of the text. But only an essentially academic, study-based critical stance would produce this question in the first place. A critical position rooted in the actualities of theatre and performance could not ask such a question: its absurdity would be clear. In an actual performance on stage it would be impossible to isolate the actor playing Hamlet, and it would be impossible to present most scenes of the play if that were the case. So the question in fact reinforces a particular critical position from which it is quite acceptable to treat performance texts in this way. All that can finally be said of it is that it is inviting a discussion of the dangers of regarding Hamlet simply as the sum total of his soliloquies. This question highlights further interesting discrepancies between text as classroom study and text as script, in so far as 'the whole play' referred to in the question can, and is, studied in the context of the classroom, but is very rarely what an audience will see on stage. The student, therefore, will be experiencing different *Hamlet*s in each different kind of encounter, but this variation of perception is not allowed for in this kind of question, and discussion of it is not invited. Instead, the classic realist position is reaffirmed – while some (misguided) people may isolate the character of Hamlet from the whole play, they are still dealing with *the* character of Hamlet in the play *Hamlet* and by implication both character and play are fixed entities.

Another characteristic of this classic realist A level approach is epitomized by reference to 'dramatic context' in the above question, which refers to the same feature of the text as that labelled 'dramatic significance', a phrase which often crops up in the questions on close textual analysis required by some examination boards, notably JMB. These are both highly intriguing ideas: what exactly do they mean? They clearly have nothing to do with the play as realized through performance, and therefore can only have meaning in the context offered by 'plot' and plot analysis undertaken in a purely academic, theoretical way. The context provided by actors on stage in a performance of the play is the real dramatic significance of the play, but discussion of this is not invited.

The pattern established at A level English is surprisingly replicated in the kinds of question asked in A level Theatre Studies, which often offer no more opportunities to think of the plays as theatre than do A level English Literature questions[5] – by and large what is offered at BA level in universities complies with the same broad description. To restate the position briefly: dramatis personae are referred to as people and often thought of as people, but are to be discussed as 'characters' deliberately created round a core of inner logic and psychological truth; Shakespeare is the author of the texts, which he produced with conscious intentionality (we are asked to evaluate his intentions and achievements); the text is not deemed to exist as a playscript for the theatre; the historical location and cultural and social determination of the text is not considered; discussion of the text is invited solely in terms of itself, or infrequently in comparison with another play of Shakespeare.

At university level, the same process as has already been described is frequently the staple fare. The same features occur. For example, dramatis personae are people: 'Macbeth, by his own actions, has robbed life of meaning'. How true is this summary of the final scene of the play?' (Birmingham BA, 1984). Shakespeare as an authoritative, intentional writer: 'Write an essay on Shakespeare's use of the theme of usurpation in either *Richard II* or *The Tempest*'. The text as an object of academic study, but rarely as a play: 'A critic has written of the "Lear Universe". Define the characteristics of the "universe" created in Shakespeare's *King Lear* by means of comparison with the universes implied in other works of literature' (while this looks like an interestingly different question, in fact its phrasing excludes consideration of the universe that can be implied by the physicality of a stage production in favour of a Platonic level of reality taken to exist elsewhere); the text as a dehistoricized, decontextualized artefact: 'Do you think Shakespeare's concern with cataclysm and self-destruction is sufficiently explained as anxiety about the maintenance of "degree" in an hierarchical society, or would you give a different account?' (here the Tillyardian emphasis in the first part of the question focuses the student on a given and learnt critical framework within which to construct an answer, although it gives an impression of being a much more open question).

Teachers who have had the opportunity to study for an MA degree will have had rather wider invitations to challenge current critical stances – 'Consider some of the achievements, and some of the shortcomings, of that tradition of Shakespearean criticism that has concerned itself with "characterisation"' (Birmingham Shakespeare Institute, MA in History of Shakespeare Criticism, 1981–1982) – but these are certainly in the minority. The inescapable conclusions to be reached from even such a brief survey as this are that teachers, as examples of students who have successfully achieved the qualifications and surmounted the hurdles provided by the British education system, have been inculcated into certain ways of seeing, understanding and teaching Shakespeare; that the weight of this system is still behind a classic realist critical stance; and that teachers having gone through this particular system feel constrained to teach Shakespeare in the same way themselves.

The classroom techniques employed to enable students to learn these responses are similarly unvaried. As Part Two makes clear, the techniques are based on the idea of static students in desks, teacher at the front in the position of power, teacher as purveyor of wisdom, knowledge and information, line-by-line examination and explication of the text involving complex 'explanations' of words and phrases, followed by essays which become, and are expected to become, more and more imbued with acceptable critical stances as the A level course proceeds – the list is depressingly familiar.

A survey of teachers in the Walsall LEA conducted during the academic year 1989–1990 bears out these conclusions.[6] Teachers were asked to respond to a range of questions about their learning and teaching experiences of Shakespeare, and the replies are very illuminating, both for what they show about the sameness of experience over a period of many years, and for what they show about the universality of experience throughout England and Wales. (As students themselves, of course, some of them had been in schools and colleges outside the Midlands.) Of the 58 teachers who responded, 50 had studied Shakespeare for O level or equivalent; 52 had studied Shakespeare at A level, and 47 had studied Shakespeare at college or university. These figures bear testimony to the pervasive presence of Shakespeare in English studies, albeit in relation to a very limited range of texts, and are also confirmatory of what we expect – it would not be 'right' for people to be teaching English who had not had some experience of Shakespeare. When we look at the nature of that experience, everything suggested by the foregoing survey is confirmed. At O and A level, teachers experienced in the classroom the reading round the class technique, coupled with some discussion, plenty of teacher notes, traditional analysis of the text, character studies and line-by-line analysis. The kind of response they were asked to make confined itself to traditional essays, character assessments, and context questions. They were certainly never asked for any kind of personal response, which throws into question the notion of personal response they will have in mind for their own students. The prevalence of the word 'traditional' in their replies, in addition to the word 'normal' (as in 'normal academic approach') makes the same point. Some experiences were positively comic, though hardly desirable: 'Shakespeare was read round the class, no discussion. Teacher often nodded off!' Few teachers mentioned any theatre visits in this context, confirming the existence of Shakespeare for these purposes as a source of words on the page solely for study in the classroom. In the context of the idealism and hope exhibited by Professor Cox and others in the Cox Report, these findings are profoundly disturbing, though hardly surprising. We are contemplating here a group of teachers of English whose teaching experience ranges from a few months to many years, who without exception demonstrate personal experience of Shakespeare in school which they can best characterize as 'traditional'. Even more disturbingly, they all know that their readers will know what 'traditional' means.

Not surprisingly, these positions are reprocessed and become the norm for their own teaching, so that for the same group of 58 teachers the kinds of experience of Shakespeare they were giving their own students at O and A level were more or less identical to what they had received as students. They themselves used phrases like 'traditional boring stuff', and 'standard essays' and 'formal' as typical of their teaching methods, although there were some glimpsees of newer, post-Leavis departures – stage technique was applied in one instance, rewriting a scene from the point of view of one character, and some use of video recordings was reported – but essentially they were teaching as they had been taught, though one or two were conscious that this was not necessarily what was best for the students. 'Personal response (asked for from students) at GCSE, greater degree of analysis and less personal response at A level, I'm afraid', says one respondent guiltily; and another says, 'Traditional as I was taught, but I hope rather more overtly dramatic', which rather conjures up images of the teacher 'acting' all over the classroom. Two respondents referred to newer approaches which they had actively sought themselves from in-service training provided within the LEA or from the Royal Shakespeare Company Education Department.[7] However, these were the exception, and it remains clear that what teachers actually do in the classroom, in this as in other instances, adheres all too strongly to their own learning experiences, unless they take active steps on their own initiative to change their classroom strategies.

With regard to their own attitudes towards Shakespeare as obligatory for Keystage 4 in the National Curriculum, the responses are worth quoting more fully. Teachers mostly feel very uncertain about this, and reflect in their responses a notion of Shakespeare for the elite, Shakespeare as 'difficult', a writer whose language is 'too difficult' for ordinary kids, and whose quality is vitiated by contact with *hoi polloi*. Questions about teachers' views of what constitutes English and literature are also raised by these responses, and most worryingly their ideas of what constitutes a 'less able' child, or a child with 'language difficulties', and their notions of what to do about this in the classroom. The current practice within schools in this LEA seems to be to deprive children of as much language as possible, and leave them with a diet of simplified and unchallenging texts which do little or nothing to awaken their linguistic curiosity.

Otherwise, a variety of responses was recorded to the invitation to note other concerns and observations about Shakespeare in the National Curriculum. One respondent felt that whoever had framed this injunction did not live in the real world, and 'won't have to teach it', which pithily sums up the responses from many teachers about the appropriateness of this new obligation. The conviction expressed here, however, that somehow pupils in the 'real world' and Shakespeare do not mix, is echoed throughout in one form or another:

> To try to read a play in its entirety would kill English for the less able, and indeed the more able, in lower school.

> Motivation of middle and lower ability classes is likely to be a major problem due to difficulties with language and the remoteness of the content.

> Forcing children to study Shakespeare regardless of their ability makes teaching very difficult and makes English lessons a chore for children who could otherwise achieve a measure of success. If Shakespeare were not forced upon children they might appreciate the plays later in life.

In principle one might agree but for certain pupils the texts are too difficult and beyond their reading abilities.

Apart from anything else, these responses indicate a view of Shakespeare whose provenance is all too clear. If you have spent your sixth-form and higher education years studying texts which are made difficult for you by the very means chosen to teach them, it is hardly surprising that you end up as a teacher convinced that such texts are not for the less able, nor even for those of average ability, and, moreover, you are convinced that the 'language' is 'difficult', is beyond pupils because by and large it is beyond you. Only those texts which you have already studied will be texts with which you feel any confidence, but they may not be what you would think of as suitable for pupils. The extreme form of this attitude is expressed here:

Apart from the highly intelligent and well-motivated pupils such as might once have been found in Grammar Schools, very few can approach Shakespeare without being alienated for life. Perhaps 'real' Shakespeare should be reserved for A Level students.

But this respondent does not like the idea of Shakespeare made easy, either, and goes on:

Certainly the linguistic difficulties are great, and the idea of watered down 'Basic English' Shakespeare is anathema.

and then goes on to ask a very pertinent question:

After all, what proportion of the population has ever had a good knowledge of his work?

This same respondent demonstrated in interview a sense of cultural ownership of Shakespeare and indeed of the whole critical process by which he had gained his own educational success, in saying that he 'did not wish it to be spoiled, nor to introduce it to kids who would not enjoy it'.

Another teacher recognizes that it will have to be done 'selectively' and in a 'stimulating manner', but thinks 'the notion of all pupils studying Shakespeare somewhat ludicrous'. It is noticeable that the emphasis in all these responses is on *studying* Shakespeare and not on what the National Curriculum statement recommended which was for all pupils to have 'some experience' of Shakespeare. In other words, their own experience has made it very difficult for all but a handful of teachers to see that there are any ways of doing anything with Shakespeare in the classroom other than studying him.

The more cynical kind of response was expressed here: 'In our school we will probably show *West Side Story* to cover these proposals!' Those attempting to feel positive about these requirements can see 'a need for more simplified versions for the less able', while others amplify the view held by the teacher quoted above: 'I am very much against re-writing Shakespeare or tinkering with the text in other ways in an attempt to make it more palatable for the unappreciative.'

The idea of Shakespeare 'readiness' was expressed by more than one respondent: 'People should read Shakespeare when they are ready for it, not because it is forced upon them in educational institutions.'

A whole cluster of attitudes is revealed by these responses but the most significant for my purposes is that group which are reflective of Shakespeare for the elite, Shakespeare being too difficult, the fear of Shakespeare being disliked by 'less able pupils' or 'spoilt' by contact with those unable to appreciate him. For these teachers he is very definitely the marker of elite status, and the sense of disbelief patently conveyed by some of them, that Shakespeare should be made accessible to all pupils, clearly indicates the uses to which Shakespeare has been put, both for these teachers and for all the generations of teachers before them.

This survey did elicit a group of more positive responses, however. There were some teachers, about a fifth of the whole group, who either felt very positive already towards the idea of experiencing Shakespeare in the classroom, or who were keen to be shown how to do it. It has to be said that the attitudes of many of this subgroup had been shaped by enthusiastic teaching which they had received as students, so while what I am saying about teachers' attitudes is generally true, there are exceptions. For those for whom this new obligation is a threat, some of the newer, active ways of experiencing Shakespeare which are referred to in the Cox Report[8] are likely to provide some positive ways forward. These methods form the basis of the discussion and investigations which constitute Part Two of this book.

PART TWO
The constructions

5 Alternative editions, alternative interpretations

In this chapter I want to discuss some of the editions currently available for use in the classroom, and to inspect not only the ways in which these editions differ, but also the ways in which they offer themselves for study, and the ways in which the kinds of approach which editors take towards each play propose a particular critical stance which by and large falls into the pattern I have discussed earlier.

Before starting this discussion, it might be useful to ask a few questions. For example, why are there so many different editions? What can each new effort add to the pool? Why do publishers calculate that a new edition is worth embarking on? How often, and for what reasons, do publishers decide to engage a new general editor to set about updating an already existing edition? Some answers can be supplied without reference to publishers themselves, simply by considering the huge market for Shakespeare plays constituted by the captive school population for A level, and the newly captive larger market produced by the situation of Shakespeare in the National Curriculum. The impact of initiatives such as the 'Shakespeare in Schools' project has also undoubtedly triggered off new and different demands for editions which take account of the critical and practical developments made since the 1970s, and the desire of publishers and educationists to inspire an adherence to Shakespeare in younger pupils has resulted in editions designed to make the study of a Shakespeare play more enjoyable. Otherwise, in view of the continued dependence of all editions on the bedrock of editing carried out in the eighteenth and nineteenth centuries (which by implication suggests that new editions are not undertaken in order to encourage editors to make startling new textual discoveries which will gather in critical plaudits for the publishing house, but rather to adapt what has already been used to current demands), there are a variety of reasons one might put forward for the plethora of editions on the market – the expansion of education since the early 1900s, the expansion of higher education and teacher training, the increase in numbers of theatre companies, the desire of publishers to keep up with each other, the current National Curriculum demands, the expansion of examinations at GCSE and A level, in both of which study of Shakespeare is required, and not least the fact that the original material has never been under any copyright and is therefore freely available for editorial use and profit.

The editions which I shall be referring to are the New Cambridge, the New Penguin, the Oxford, the Alexander, the New Swan Shakespeare, the Arden, and the Folger Library Shakespeare.[1] These seven editions constitute only a fraction of the total number currently in print. A recent count yielded 20 English editions (in the sense of having been produced mainly for consumption in Britain, by publishing houses that were, or still are, predominantly British-owned) which comprise anything from twelve of the plays to the whole canon in single volumes, and at least five editions of the complete works. Exactly what different functions can all these editions perform? What different parts of the market can they appeal to? In examining these editions I shall be looking at the ways in which they differ in stated purpose; in their treatment of the text itself with regard to spelling, textual ambiguities and cruxes, and punctuation; their editorial provenance; the kinds of notes they provide; and the ways in which they treat 'uncomfortable' aspects of the texts.

It might be in order here to discuss briefly why the plays of Shakespeare produce such problems for editors. When we are not specifically considering problems of editing and textual dependability, most of us involved in teaching Shakespeare disregard these aspects of the text, and concentrate instead on making as much meaning as possible of the particular edition of the text we are using with our students. Very rarely are these considerations made part of the assessment objectives of any examination, and only at higher degree level do students consider them. However, they are of central importance: to be understood as producing the essential instability of the texts, and therefore the essential impossibility of constructing a 'real', 'proper', 'genuine' text. The production of the texts in the first place was the outcome of a mixture of separate elements: one was the Quarto editions themselves which were produced for profit (surprisingly, plays only constituted 1.5 per cent of the book trade in the early seventeenth century, which was not geared to the production and selling of plays: on average, only three new dramatic plays were printed and sold every year); another was foul papers, which by and large, were the corrected drafts or working copies; a third was the prompt books, and the last was the memory of individuals involved in the staging of the plays. The collation and interpretation of these elements was in itself an editorial process, and it culminated in the first collected Folio publication of the works, brought out by John Heminge and Henry Condell in 1623, as an 'office of their care and paine'.[2] When consideration is also given to the ways in which the actual printing of the texts was undertaken at the time, both during and after Shakespeare's professional career, it becomes evident that the whole process is shot through with uncertainties, ambiguities, inaccuracies and downright carelessness.

If we consider, as an example, the situation in which the first quarto printing of *King Lear* took place, we might begin to appreciate why the texts are so unstable. We have to conjure up in our minds 4 January 1608, at eight o'clock in the morning, in a printing house on Fleet Street, perfumed by the odours from the nearby River Fleet, used as an open sewer, with the Thames frozen solid. Nicholas Oakes, a young printer of 27, is just beginning to set up the presses with the help of an adult compositor and his apprentice, and an adult journeyman and his apprentice, for the printing of a new play, *King Lear*, the first play he has printed. The laborious nature of the work to some extent explains some of the problems we now have in deciding what was the most likely word or phrase in the original. It involved setting up the forme of type metal for each quarto sheet, working out how much of the text would go onto what would turn out to be each individual page of the finished volume, fitting in the verse accurately (although sometimes to fill up a badly calculated page you might decide to split verse lines in half to produce enough material to fill your page; conversely, you might double up lines of a song, for instance, in order to make space for the rest of the page), working in the freezing cold in the inadequate light seeping through the oiled paper windows, with the perpetual smell in your nostrils of the lye used for cleaning the ink off the type metal, and not least the difficulties of reading and interpreting the papers from which the text is being composed. The actual process of printing once the forme has been set up is itself slow and hard, and by this method of hand printing only about 1200 sheets a day are produced.[3]

There is additional useful material on the ways in which the printer corrected the type already in a forme, and how it was possible to produce and bind a copy of a play from both corrected and uncorrected sheets, in the 'Account of the Text' of the New Penguin edition of the play. Bearing in mind all this information, it is easy to see why the text cannot be taken as a fixed entity. Textual work is constantly being undertaken not only on 'correct' versions of this play, and others, but also on comparisons between Quarto and Folio texts, and between so-called 'good' and 'bad' Quartos. Variations between the First and Second Quarto editions of three of the plays, *Romeo and Juliet, Hamlet* and *Henry V*, for example, show as much as a 33 per cent change in the script from one edition to the second. It is being suggested quite forcefully, by Steven Urkowitz[4] among others, that these comparisons yield many useful and interesting insights into the interrelatedness of these different versions of the plays, into the significances and uncertainties of the texts revealed by this form of comparative study, and that they point to the inconclusive results of the whole undertaking. The texts are unstable, and the more work like this is done, the more incontestable becomes this position.

The challenge facing each new contemporary editor is not simply the enormous task inherent in editing a Shakespeare play, with all the attendant textual choices outlined above, and the need to operate within the already established editorial framework of the particular publisher; but the requirement to construct the whole within a critical approach which speaks to a contemporary readership largely composed of teachers, students, academics and theatre companies. These potential audiences to a large extent dictate the format of the edition. Even where this intended readership is not referred to, it is possible to adduce the kind of reader the editor had in mind. For example, the New Swan Shakespeare starts with a Foreword by the General Editor, Bernard Lott, in which he states that:

> The aim of this edition of *Hamlet* is to ensure that the reader fully understands and appreciates the play . . . the explanations are simple in language, and avoid the long expositions to be found in some editions . . .

implying that the edition is aimed at students, either of A-level English or certainly of English at a pre-degree stage, an assumption borne out by the name of the series, *Advanced*. What this says about this editor's view of Shakespeare and of his critical stance can be left for analysis until later. The somewhat coercive statement involving use of the words 'ensure', 'fully understands' and 'appreciates' betrays a particular kind of attitude not expressed by other editors, implying as it does that full understanding is possible, and appearing to claim that an editor's efforts can actually 'ensure' understanding.

In contrast to this, the Arden Shakespeare General Editor, Una Ellis-Fermor, in the *King Lear* edition of 1952, makes a statement outlining a diffidence of approach, a modesty of claim:

> Much has happened in the last fifty years, through the great extension of palaeographical, bibliographical and textual scholarship; and our better understanding of (among other things) the nature and relations of Folio and Quarto texts has led us not always into more certainty, but sometimes rather into wholesome and chastened uncertainty . . . Some of us [editors of individual plays] may prove to have solved these [problems of each text] in a way which posterity will repudiate.

While no particular reader is described here, the publisher is quite clear about potential buyers and claims in the blurb on the back cover:

> For the general reader and for students who want something more substantial then school texts or a one-volume Shakespeare, the Arden edition, edited to the highest standards of modern scholarship, has continued to prove invaluable.

There is an implication here about 'school texts' which suggests that they are simple, superficial and lacking in critical and explanatory material, that they are somehow not quite the thing for the *serious* reader.

Much earlier editors, like W.J. Craig, in charge of the Oxford University Press edition of the complete works of 1911, explains his editorial decisions without reference either to a putative readership or to any stated purpose in the editing other than to make the texts more accessible to the general reader by revising the punctuation of previous editions and 'to increase the ease of reference I have numbered the lines at shorter intervals than have been adopted hitherto'.

This collected works edition by the Oxford University Press illustrates very well the shift in thinking about Shakespeare and the change in appropriate verbal forms in which to describe his works, since the early years of the century. The General Introduction to this collected edition is by Swinburne, who indulges in what seems to us in the 1990s as an overblown rhetoric in his eulogizing of Shakespeare. Although I have already quoted him in Chapter 1, he is worth quoting again to restate the editorial stance deemed appropriate at that time:

> The word Shakespeare connotes more than any other man's name that ever was written or spoken upon earth ... All that can be known of manhood, of womanhood, and of childhood, he knew better than any other man ever born. It is not only the crowning glory of England, it is the crowning glory of mankind, that such a man should ever have been born as William Shakespeare.

This is patent nonsense to us now, but the emotional charge behind these words, and the ensuing cultural reverberations are still with us, and indeed have played their part in putting Shakespeare into the National Curriculum. In contrast, the Prefatory Note to the Alexander edition states straightforwardly:

> By keeping in mind the fact that the language has changed considerably in four hundred years, as have the customs, jokes, and the stage conventions, the editors have aimed at helping the modern reader − whether English is his mother tongue or not − to grasp the full significance of these plays. The Notes, intended primarily for examination candidates, are presented in a simple direct style. The needs of those unfamiliar with British culture have been specially considered.

Of the editions being considered this is the only one which states its intended readership so clearly, and is the only preface which acknowledges that Shakespeare forms an integral part of English qualifying examinations open to foreign and overseas students. However, this praiseworthy perception is somewhat vitiated by the reference to the reader as 'he', and by the notion, echoing the New Swan quoted above, that it is possible to grasp the 'full significance' of the plays. This indicates again a particular critical and ideological stance, found expressed in the introductions and choice of notes of nearly all these editions.

However, this Preface does note something which the A.C. Bradley school of thought studiously avoids,

> Since quiet study of the printed word is unlikely to bring fully to life plays that were written directly for the public theatre, attention has been drawn to dramatic effects which are important in performance. The editors see Shakespeare's plays as living works of art which can be enjoyed today on stage, film and television in many parts of the world.

The editorial cast of mind which attempts to explain and explicate is exemplified in this opening to the Folger Library Shakespeare:

> Designed to make Shakespeare's classic plays available to the general reader, each edition contains a reliable text with modernized spelling and punctuation, scene-

by-scene plot summaries, and explanatory notes clarifying obscure and obsolete expressions.

The general reader can be taken here to be one who cannot be expected to take readily or with much understanding to Shakespeare's language but who nevertheless wants to read the plays. Within the American educational establishment this may be more taken for granted than in Britain, where, unlike in America, it is not the case that high school students would have read at least three of the plays, and therefore might become those general readers for whom the edition is intended. What is revealing about this introduction is the felt necessity to 'modernize' and the idea of obsolescence in language.

There are editions which make no general statements about their intentions, such as the New Cambridge, which is more concerned in any prefatory notes to explain details of editors and editing, and the New Penguin, which provides only the editorial introductions to each specific text.

All the editions being considered offer modern spelling, and I have not been able to find many obvious differences, but differences in punctuation are much more noticeable, and indeed the whole use of printing variables to communicate the text is noticeably different between editions. These uses of punctuation are almost entirely later additions to the scripts: the original quartos contain only minimal punctuation. There was little at the end of verse lines, which were taken as a form of punctuation in their own right, and only occasionally were commas used to indicate pauses over and above those understood from the verse layout itself. I want to use Edmund's speech in *King Lear*, 'Thou Nature art my goddess', to compare uses of punctuation in different editions, and quote in full the New Penguin version:

Thou, Nature, art my goddess; to thy law
My services are bound. Wherefore should I
Stand in the plague of custom and permit
The curiosity of nations to deprive me,
For that I am some twelve or fourteen moonshines
Lag of a brother? Why bastard? Wherefore base?
When my dimensions are as well-compact,
My mind as generous, and my shape as true
As honest madam's issue? Why brand they us
With 'base'? with 'baseness'? 'bastardy'? 'base, base'?
Who in the lusty stealth of nature take
More composition and fierce quality
Than doth within a dull, stale, tired bed
Go to the creating a whole tribe of fops
Got 'tween asleep and wake? Well then
Legitimate Edgar, I must have your land.
Our father's love is to the bastard Edmund
As to the legitimate. Fine word 'legitimate'!
Well, my 'legitimate', if this letter speed

And my invention thrive, Edmund the base
Shall top the legitimate. I grow. I prosper.
Now gods stand up for bastards![5]

This edition, in common with many other New Penguin volumes, removes as much punctuation as possible in the interests of clarity and flow of the line. The editor, G.K. Hunter, has used the Folio text here, unless Quarto variants, both corrected and uncorrected, have been thought superior. In contrast, the Arden edition (which is also based on the Folio edition, 'but . . . we shall accept Quarto readings not only where the Folio readings are manifestly corrupt, but also where the Quarto seems palpably superior') punctuates the speech more fully, for example:

My mind as generous, and my shape as true,
As honest madam's issue?

where the comma after 'true' has the effect of equalizing the weight of the three instances of the word 'as' and forcing emphasis onto the words 'generous', 'true' and 'honest'. In contrast, the New Penguin's lack of a comma encourages the flow of the comparison, focuses on the words 'as true as' and tends to throw the weight of the emphasis onto 'mind', 'shape' and 'issue'. In the New Penguin version 'as true as' becomes the fulcrum of a balance between two lines and two groups of ideas. In the Arden version the claim being expressed by Edmund is split into three parts by the use of this comma. In another example from the speech, where the New Penguin has the words 'base', 'baseness' and 'bastardy' in speech marks to indicate and allude to the very voices using those words about people like himself, the Arden edition omits speech marks. This has the effect of turning the words simply into referents for those ideas and concepts, and dephysicalizing the experience which Edmund is expressing. The New Penguin version gives the actor a palpable clue to the delivery of this line – the speech marks turn the words into the taunts and scorn of remembered voices. This usage is of a piece with the editor's remarks in 'An Account of the Text' at the end of the volume, where he says: 'I assume that this is a play in which the physical relationship of person to person and the range of significant gesture are very important, and often far from obvious.'

In another example from the speech, the Arden edition has 'well compact' instead of 'well-compact' which turns the phrase into a qualifier and a signifier, rather than a signifier composed of two ideas. The New Penguin edition here is producing one idea only for each of the instances of the word 'as', so that the lines give us in sequence 'as well-compact', 'as generous', 'as true' and 'as honest', in contrast to the Arden where this balance is not established to include this coinage. In speaking the speech, the Arden two-word version asks for equal emphasis on each of the words 'as', 'well' and 'compact', while the New Penguin version throws the emphasis onto the second syllable of 'compact'.

The incidence of different punctuation styles is well illustrated by this speech, and there are similar divergences in many other parts of the text between the two editions; not, however, between all editions. The Oxford edition is closer to the Arden, except for its use of 'the' in '*the* creating' and '*the* legitimate' where the Arden has 'th''. This difference is an example of editors trying to find ways of accounting for the wrong number of syllables in the two lines, and attempting to rectify their scansion. The significance of these variations of punctuation lies in the areas I have outlined: emphasis, speaking aloud and acting; and such variations can have profound effects on the kind of active work to be undertaken with students which is described in a later chapter. What they also show very clearly, even if one knows nothing of printing or textual history, is that there is no such thing as a 'correct' version of any of the texts.

Editions differ in their treatment of textual difficulties and cruxes, and the decisions made by editors reveal the particular cultural and critical pressures under which they are working. For example, an edition aimed mainly at students will gloss over the editorial decisions made over particular cruxes, and will often gloss over the meaning of words which may be differently printed in different versions. *Hamlet* provides an instructive example here. In his soliloquy after the player's 'Hecuba' speech, Hamlet castigates himself for his inaction, and talks of unpacking 'his heart with words' like 'a whore', and 'fall a-cursing like a very drab,/ A stallion!' This New Penguin version of the line is in contrast to the New Swan and the Oxford editions, both of which have 'scullion'. These variants illustrate several aspects of the editing problem, but, most prominently perhaps, they also illustrate the cultural bias of the editor. The New Penguin editor, Professor T.J.B. Spencer, explains in his note to this line why he chooses 'stallion': '*stallion* a prostitute (like *drab*). F [Folio] reads "Scullion", an acceptable reading sometimes preferred by editors. But *whore* and *drab* perhaps lead naturally to *stallion*.' Professor Spencer is prepared to acknowledge the implications of these sexually explicit words in his note, and in so doing draws further attention to their function in the text. The other two editors fight shy of this. In the New Swan, which is laid out with notes on facing pages to text, there is no note or explanation at all for 'scullion', and in the Oxford edition the word 'scullion' appears in the glossary meaning 'a servant who performed the menial duties of the kitchen'. However, 'scullion' could also mean a 'whore, linked to foul anal smells. "An abusive epithet" (*OED*)',[6] and the New Penguin use of 'stallion' turns out to be unnecessary to convey this particular meaning. But, only the New Penguin edition shows any interest in making this meaning overt, while the two other editions efface this layer of significance, and continue to present Shakespeare shorn of his sexual innuendoes and references where they can manage to do this without cutting the text. These editorial choices in vocabulary, and then in notes, promote a particular, culturally signified version of the plays.

Similarly, patently sexual references in the plays, such as Hamlet's question to Ophelia about whether he should lie in her lap, and whether she thinks he meant 'country matters', are not even noted in the Oxford and New Swan editions, although the New Penguin continues its open and helpful attitude by explaining that this means sexual intercourse. One is left feeling that these editorial interventions and decisions are to do with editors more often than not having their own psychological and ideological problems with these aspects of Shakespeare. How can he be the greatest playwright ever, the national icon of the English, if he descends so alarmingly into this kind of sexual explicitness? This is just 'not British', and while they may not cut the offending parts out, many pretend they are not there by making no reference whatever to them, either in their notes or in their own editorial material.

This huge area of editorial decision-making, the decisions made with regard to the sexual and bawdy meanings of words and phrases in the texts, makes a fascinating subject of study. Not surprisingly, editorial attitudes are dictated by personal preference and outlook, the view held of likely reader response, ideas of 'correctness' and what is acceptable, and in some cases what will be allowed by education officials. In the USA, for example, there exist 'Standard School Abridgement' versions of the most commonly studied plays. *Romeo and Juliet* is deprived of *all* references to parts of the body, including feet, legs, wombs, bones, hams, bosom; all references to God, Jesus, religion, heretics, liars, hell, fiend; all the obvious bawdy and sexual words such as prick, flesh, maidenhood, Cupid, Venus, and all Mercutio's references to historical women thought of as famous lovers, the Nurse's talk of bearing burdens at night, women growing by men, love itself, maiden, whoreson, kisses; and the whole of the short scene with the musicians. This censorship leads to extraordinary excisions such as the removal of half of Friar Laurence's speech about Nature, as it is couched in the extended metaphor of Nature as a woman; and deprives the play of all but the faintest hint of any sexuality. In studying *Romeo and Juliet* this seems perverse to say the least. Of course, this is nothing new, and has existed in Britain in the form of abridged versions designed for innocent school pupils for a very long time. However, this American version is enforced in some states; it is the version which you must do if you wish to study the play with high school students. Whatever one's view of Shakespeare's bawdy and sexual meanings, what play are you studying if you study the Standard School Abridgement version of *Romeo and Juliet*? It is certainly nothing like the play Shakespeare would recognize, and can hardly be said to be *Romeo and Juliet* at all. So, what is it?

The critical stance taken by editors, which has of course informed the whole process of their editorship, is most clearly expressed in their introductions, and is also to be recognized in the notes and explanations furnished with the text. To exemplify what I want to say here I shall use two versions of the text of *King Lear*, which bear some relationship to each other in that the editor of one, the Arden Shakespeare's Kenneth Muir, expresses indebtedness to the editor of the other, the New Penguin's Professor G.K. Hunter. The layout and presentation of each version follows the pattern established by each publisher.

The Arden edition offers a very long introduction, divided into sections on the text, the date of the play, sources, the play, and recent criticism where references have been updated since the first publication of this edition in 1964 by a postscript added in 1978. This is followed by the text, which is printed on the top part of each page, the bottom part being taken up with appropriate notes. The notes include textual variants as well as explanations and allusions, with copious references to previous editors. The alternatives to be derived from earlier editions are made explicit. The text is followed by seven appendices which quote passages and extracts from source or related material.

The critical position taken by Kenneth Muir is one that could be characterized as 'traditional': that is, it is still heavily dependent on nineteenth-century and earlier critics – or rather, sees it as a necessity to quote their thoughts about, for example, the playability of the text – and confronts the critical position of A.C. Bradley rather then pushing beyond his position. It is therefore a very academically rooted approach, cautiously producing counter-arguments to the notion that *King Lear* cannot be acted, but still very dependent on Bradley as the *Ur*-critic to be acknowledged. Muir spends some time analysing Bradley's objections to the play on the grounds that it is 'theatrically weak', and accepts this as a debating position even though he knows that Bradley never saw the play in performance. The continuing power of the Bradley line of argument is astonishing, certainly for the 1990s, but perhaps less so for the 1960s. What is equally surprising is the apparent necessity to discuss the Bradley line at all, and even to question the text as a piece for the theatre. It is, therefore, very much in the tradition of Shakespeare in the study that this introductory material is couched. Other characteristics of this essentially classic realist approach are reproduced. The dramatis personae are discussed as though they are real people: 'Edgar, in real life, would perhaps have revealed himself to his father; . . . He had wished, we may suppose, not only to overcome his father's desire for suicide, but also to convince him that the gods were not spiteful.' The author is not only in complete control of what he is writing, but it is possible to deduce the kind of mood he was in while he was engaged in composition and also to know his attitudes to religion, among other things: 'Shakespeare was certainly in a ruthless mood when he wrote *King Lear*, and his religious attitude provides no easy comfort, and makes no concessions to sentimentality.'

The discussion of sources is very wide-ranging, but there is no discussion of the play as a historically located construction; sources are all deemed to be entirely literary, narratives couched in varying forms, and in this regard the play is implied to have sprung out of a kind of limbo. The attitude to sexual references is to smother them under superficially convincing explanations. Thus, Lear's attack on women, in Act IV, scene 6, which includes the line 'Whose face between her forks presages snow' is coyly explained as 'who seems to be frigidly chaste' with an additional allusion to a nineteenth-century suggestion that 'forks' means 'instruments for keeping up women's hair'. (This is nothing compared to the Oxford edition, which can only just bring itself to explain that forks are 'the lower limbs'.) The iteration throughout Lear's speech of words denoting sexual depravity and excessive appetite, and the strength of the attack, is played down by this 'gentlemanly' explication.

The New Penguin edition provides an introduction of 45 pages, with additional notes on 'Further Reading on Editions', sources and criticism. The Commentary on the text, which follows the text, takes up 127 pages compared to the text's 128 pages. The Commentary is followed by 'An Account of the Text' and 'Words for Music in *King Lear*'. The editor moves his consideration of the play away from the central figure of Lear, and focuses instead on the play as a whole, for which, he says: 'What seems to be needed is a description of the play which relates plot to meaning in such a way that the two dimensions support each other.' He takes the view that a search for the 'meaning' of the play is essentially irrelevant, that the search for 'messages' yields only the obvious, whereas, in his view, the play presents us with 'a terrifying maelstrom of words and images that express man's need to see himself as meaningful'. This stance is some distance from that exemplified by the Bradley school of thought, and yet it is still noticeably working within the classic realist mode. In particular, Shakespeare is the authoritative writer, who

> went to some pains to create the image of a society which had not yet received the Christian revelation. His art is usually quite happy to be anachronistic ... He seems to have wished to explore, with almost scientific thoroughness, the problem of Providence in a context which does not exact the Christian answer.

Much of the discussion of the play in the introduction is conducted in terms of Shakespeare's intention, which ultimately undermines the validity of the analysis.

For all the mixture of critical positions being taken in this introduction, this editor does recognize the necessity to acknowledge aspects of the play suppressed in the Arden edition. For the same speech of Lear's examined above, this edition's notes are quite explicit:

> The key distinction throughout the speech is between 'natural' or illegal sexuality, which gradually moves from *Adultery, lecher, copulation*, to the more violent representation of *luxury, pell-mell, riotous appetite*, and [on the other hand] the legal proprieties embodied in the *King*, the *lawful sheets*, the *women all above*.

The specific line 'Whose face between her forks presages snow' is explained by: 'Her *forks* are her legs. Her face *presages* or indicates that the other face *between her forks* is frigid or chaste.'

Unlike the Arden edition, this New Penguin pays a great deal of attention to the text as a play, and provides eight pages of introductory notes devoted to the play in performance. This goes some way to enabling the reader to see the text as unfixed, capable of being shaped to suit each new generation, and therefore unstable and available for constant reinterpretation and representation. It is the New Penguin edition of the plays which is used by companies like the Royal Shakespeare Company, an acknowledgement of its recognition that the plays are plays.

Analysis of these different editions does point up the difficult line to be trodden by editors between unnecessary display of their own academic scholarship and oversimplification of textual challenges in the interests of popularization. It also points up the reluctance of many academic editors to make any attempt to treat the texts as pieces for the theatre, or to consider them in any context of performance. There are, however, editions which have been produced specifically for schools, among which is a new *Illustrated Shakespeare Series* published by Stanley Thornes in 1989, which does attempt to emphasize the theatrical existence of the plays. The editorial material in these editions is scanty, and no explanation of textual provenance is given, but their virtue is their attempt to present the texts in conjunction with images of dramatic action: each page has illustrations to accompany specific lines of the text, taken from drawn or photographed moments in theatre productions ranging in date from 1822 to 1989. The editor, Neil King, remarks: 'One of the guiding principles of this edition is that the student must have some idea of the play in performance . . . A literary experience of a play is only valid after a theatrical one.' This sounds very promising: the editions are designed particularly for GCSE students, and also contain brief notes on each page side by side with the text, and some suggestions for written, oral and drama work on many pages. The editor offers sixty 'Activities and Questions' at the end of the text. However, the edition is caught in the trap of trying to cover too many of the possibilities, and difficulties, thrown up by the text. The pages are overloaded with information, both visual and textual, the format makes the individual copies too big to use easily in any active work, and the teacher needs to be very clear about which aspect of each page is going to be ingested first. Text by no means dominates the page.

This edition exemplifies many of the problems and evasions already discussed, and the editor reveals his essentially desk-bound approach to the text: 'the student must be able to produce the play in his or her own mind before close study of the text is possible'. This, however, is the result of working within the constraints imposed by the perceived demands of GCSE English Literature. It seems that in attempting to cater for examination requirements, of whatever kind, even the most enlightened editor is forced back into strategies for enhancing study of the text. In this case the dressing up of the text does have some interesting effects: while the text itself is treated as a fixed thing to have literal meaning made of it, the illustrations paradoxically show how unstable and open to a range of theatrical interpretations it is. They include photographs of a black theatre company in performance, which add to the many possibilities for investigation offered by this particular presentation of the text, but which are not exploited by the editor in his suggestions for work. This edition appears to fail to recognize its own significance. It does show vividly how the demands of an examination syllabus, however freely defined, produce the familiar compulsion to 'study the text closely', and how they close down many of the physical learning experiences inherent in the text.

In spite of the existence of editions like this, which emphasize and acknowledge the visual and theatrical nature of the plays, the current common situation of Shakespeare in schools and universities remains by and large in a desk-bound state, giving little incentive to editors to work from any other perspectives.

6 Shakespeare and video

Video Shakespeare is the only experience that many pupils will ever have of the works of the Bard. Video is now common in English classrooms, where 'seeing the video' has become equated with 'doing' the book. Some of the implications of this practice, of media studies as an analytical tool largely unknown to English teachers, and of the existence of Shakespeare on video, need to be discussed. It is questionable to what extent the fundamental significance of these potentially huge areas of investigation is recognized by teachers as they settle down with their class to watch Franco Zeffirelli's *Romeo and Juliet* to comply with the National Curriculum stipulation that pupils 'should experience some of the works of Shakespeare'.

Media Studies is peculiarly subject to definitions and redefinitions as a curriculum area. Its current position reflects its past history, and particularly the attitudes taken towards it. The media as an area for concern and/or study was already being referred to in pejorative terms in the Spens Report on Secondary Education in 1938 which spoke of the ways in which the 'rising generation' was being 'subtly corrupted' by hoardings, cinema and the press, and exhibited such concern at the 'infectious accent of Hollywood' that it advocated speech training as a way of combating this baleful influence.[1] Interestingly, speech training was also being promoted in Britain as a way of abolishing class barriers. No need to speculate about whose speech pupils would be trained in. The ideological stance behind this statement, deriving from the liberal-humanist tradition, and taking for granted the superiority and desirability of the speech habits and cultural stance of dominant bourgeois groups, is reflective of a position formulated by F.R. Leavis and Denys Thompson in *Culture and Environment*, first published in the 1930s but still powerfully influencing English teachers and English teaching in the 1950s, and 1960s.[2] Residual elements of this ideological position, which among other things believes in the moral and beatifying properties of 'literature', advocated with a proselytizing zeal, and which turns teachers into missionaries, still prevail in the rationale about their role held by English teachers. The following from Leavis and Thompson, in an attenuated form, still informs a range of attitudes in the classroom:

> Those who in school are offered (perhaps) the beginnings of education in taste are
> exposed, out of school, to the competing exploitation of the cheapest emotional
> responses; films, newspapers, publicity in all its forms, commercially-catered fiction
> – all offer satisfaction at the lowest level, and inculcate the choosing of the most
> immediate pleasures, got with the least effort.

The teacher, one of the 'many intelligent men and women who every year go into schools', has a priest-like role in education:

> In a world of depressed and cynical aimlessness there is for them work that, aiming
> at considerable and considered ends, will yield enough in immediate effect to make
> whole-hearted devotion possible . . . we are committed to more consciousness; that
> way, if any, lies salvation. We cannot, as we might in a healthy state of culture,
> leave the citizen to be formed unconsciously by his environment; if anything like a
> worthy idea of satisfactory living is to be saved, he must be trained to discriminate
> and resist.

For all the moral righteousness of this, it has been pointed out that media work would never have begun in the classroom had attention not been drawn to the 'dangers' of the media, within such a framing device.[3] The moral tone established the necessary basis, for the time. During the 1960s attitudes towards media work continued to evolve, lurching along the way through pro-film but anti-television stances, as implied in the following from the Newsom Report of 1963:[4]

> We need to train children to look critically and discriminate between what is good
> and bad in what they see. They must learn to realise that many makers of films and
> of television programmes present false or distorted views of people, relationships,
> and experience in general, besides producing much trivial and worthless stuff made
> according to stock patterns. By presenting examples of films selected for the
> integrity of their treatment of human values, and the craftsmanship with which they
> were made, alongside others of mixed or poor quality, we cannot only build up a
> way of evaluating but also lead the pupils to an understanding of film as a unique
> and potentially valuable art form in its own right as capable of communi-
> cating depth of experience as any other art form.

The linking together here of film and television, and the failure to suggest a critique for the study of television (notice how the word 'television' disappears from the paragraph), while film is accorded a range of critical touchstones – integrity, human values, valuable art form, false or distorted views, craftsmanship – contributed to a situation where teachers began to use film with more confidence in the classroom. The responses from pupils being aimed for were closely underpinned by the kind of aesthetic outlined in Newsom, while they omitted television from the syllabus.

During the 1970s a survey of teacher attitudes to teaching television revealed that:

> A considerable number of English teachers said that their main aim in introducing
> mass media into lessons was to point out the 'dangers' of the media and to provide
> pupils with a 'defence'. Of the English teachers who answered our question, 36 per
> cent answered along these lines . . . This attitude is far more common among
> English teachers than among teachers of other subjects.[5]

The writers of the survey pinpoint the view of the media still commonly held by
English teachers at the time of the survey (which incidentally demonstrates the
strength and endurance of the Leavisite position and opens up questions of what
has been going on in teacher training since the 1960s), which consistently ignores
what pupils are actually doing in their television watching, and the degree of
sophistication they bring to their choices and judgements:

> The 'Zombie' view [that is the view that media audiences are 'captive and
> defenceless "Zombies"'] and its concommitant stress on the need to inoculate
> pupils against media influences, together with the emphasis on upholding the
> superiority of literary culture appear to provide the perspective of a number of
> English teachers.

Official reports, such as those already referred to, as well as the Bullock Report
and the Cox Report,[6] show an increasing confidence in knowing what they mean
by media education, and increasingly press for its inclusion in the English syllabus. The Bullock Report recognized the need for atttention to be paid to television in the English classroom, and attempted to redress the balance, but was
unable to suggest anything more precise than the following: 'Although there is
unquestioned value in developing a critical approach to television, as to listening
and reading, we would place the emphasis on deepening the pupils' appreciation',[7] which it is suggested can be brought about by the kind of group or individual study of a television programme or text which might compare it with
treatment of the same theme in other media, or some study of television as a
medium coupled with exploration of methods of production. One does not find
here any critical or philosophical standpoint from which the whole matter might
be addressed, and this lack suggests that the tools with which to do this were
unfamiliar to the committee.

Within a very unevenly developing situation, where the most advanced
practitioners were beginning to apply descriptive and investigatory procedures to
work on television, rather than the evaluative appraisals of the past, there still
remained a strong antipathy toward television, characterized by Len Masterman
thus:

> Most fundamentally, there persists to this day in English studies – it is apparent in
> even the most liberal formulations – a deeply-rooted distrust of the mass media, and
> particularly television, as prime agents of cultural debasement and decline.[8]

He discerns a second, equally disquieting feature:

> The second constant theme in the shifting relationship between English teaching
> and the mass media concerns the reluctance of those teachers who have taken the

media seriously to unload very much of the critical baggage acquired during their literary training . . . television is not ersazt literature, and is not best understood through the application of aesthetic or moral criteria having their roots in literary or even film criticism . . . it may not be best understood through the attempt to apply *any* kind of evaluative criteria.

As I shall go on to discuss in a later section of this chapter, the possibilities for collision between literary, evaluative criteria and the more investigative approach advocated here by Masterman are central to any consideration of literary texts on television.

The Cox Report in 1989 appeared after several years of a government which encouraged a nation-wide push by the DES to establish computers in all schools, and a constantly reiterated imperative to provide education skewed towards a technical, vocationally-oriented curriculum for pupils aged 14–16, with an accompanying emphasis on information technology. These factors had in some ways changed the whole general attitude among teachers towards technology, and under that umbrella towards television. Cox felt confident in quoting the following from Cary Bazalgette[9] assuming that its meanings would be taken up by readers of the Report:

> Media education seeks to increase children's critical understanding of the media – namely, television, film, radio, photography, popular music, printed materials, and computer software. How they work, how they produce meaning, how they are organised and how audiences make sense of them, are the issues that media education addresses. [It] aims to develop systematically children's critical and creative powers through analysis and production of media artefacts. This also deepens their understanding of the pleasure and enjoyment provided by the media. Media education aims to create more active and critical media users who will demand, and could contribute to, a greater range and diversity of media products.

The Report follows its predecessor in making explicit its view that media education is important:

> We have considered media education largely as part of the exploration of contemporary culture, alongside more traditional literary texts. And we emphasise elsewhere that the concepts of text and genre should be broadly interpreted in English. Television and film form substantial parts of pupils' experience out of school and teachers need to take this into account. Pupils should have the opportunity to apply their critical faculties to these major parts of contemporary culture.

This general approach emerges almost intact in *English in the National Curriculum* (1989) where it informs the statements on media education which appear in the Non-Statutory Guidance for English issued by the National Curriculum Council.[10] Within the National Curriculum, media education is seen both as the province of English teachers, and as a cross-syllabus element:

> Media education contributes to most aspects of the English curriculum. Practical and analytical work on the media will involve negotiation, problem-solving, group

decision-making, selection and editing, all of which enhance children's abilities in reading, writing, speaking and listening.[11]

The Cox Report does appear to have shifted the approach to television away from the evaluative and into the descriptive and investigative realms advocated by Masterman. This approach is the only one which will move work on television into areas that open up critical awareness, and one which provides the necessary critical vocabulary, unfortunately not supplied in *English in the National Curriculum*. We might be getting somewhere if teachers of English were conversant with the ideas contained in the following:

> [All] programmes need elucidation, all need to be read as cultural texts, iconic in character, which can be decoded to reveal large numbers of meanings. The codings themselves will reveal and embody the ideology and professional practices of the broadcasting institutions, demonstrate the constructed and mediated nature of the 'normal' world of the programmes, and invite a comparison with other possible, but suppressed codings. It is with cultural criticism in this sense that the study of television should be concerned.[12]

The ability to apply these criteria to television, and to make active use of them with pupils in the classroom is still limited to relatively few English teachers. The reasons outlined above explain this situation: the uncertainty and outright hostility of English teachers in the past to the idea of Media Studies means that very often such studies have become the province of Social Studies departments; because little thought and training have been given to English teachers in this area, their own attachment to the critical vocabulary and stance of their literary training has tended to prolong this mistrust; because they are inexperienced and therefore lack the kind of critical base indicated in Masterman's statement above, they face the same difficulties now, in spite of the clear requirement in the National Curriculum to include media work in the daily classroom experience of pupils.

Against this background of very diverse provision across schools, we must set the actual televisual material with which we are concerned. The relationship of a video recording to a television production, and of both to a Shakespeare play, is a very complex one. The process of construction of each of these versions is of particular importance. We have a variety of possibilities of provenance when we talk about Shakespeare on video: a play which was originally produced in the theatre, has been recast for television in terms of set and setting, movements, physical relationships in the playing space, gesture, facial expressions for close-ups, and voice production; a play which was originally produced in the theatre and has been recast for filming, where the film has then been shown on television, or has been produced on video; a play which was originally conceived as a film production with all that that implies in terms of cuts, changes, setting and the actual film techniques used, which has been shown on television and has also been recorded on video; a production that was originally conceived for television and has then been recorded on video; a production that was conceived for television with the built-in intention that the production would be available for sale as a video recording. Examples of all these variants exist. The questions to be considered here are, what are the relationships between these different versions of the plays, particularly those undergoing transformation from one medium to another? What are the differences between these different versions? And what light can any critique of this process throw on the study of Shakespeare on video?

The history of Shakespeare on film is surprisingly long, going back at least to Hollywood versions of some of the plays in the 1920s and 1930s in black and white, and including the more recent Olivier films of *Henry V*, *Hamlet* and *Richard III*, Polanski's film of *Macbeth*, Zeffirelli's version of *Romeo and Juliet*, and Derek Jarman's version of *The Tempest*. Russian and Japanese versions of the plays, most notably by the Japanese director, Kurosawa, are radical adaptations of the plays for the screen, and literally treat the printed text as one from which to make a reinterpretation. (In the category of filmed Shakespeare I am not including filmed stage productions.) All sorts of treatments are given the plays in these versions, including substantial cutting and rearranging of the printed text, the actors speaking in Russian or Japanese (which casts the whole experience into a quite alien mode), and some form of naturalistic setting operating as the physical framework for the action. The features they have in common are that they were all conceived for the cinema, and that the camera controls all responses from the audience – 'when the eye is directed unaccountably towards one set of characters, excluding all the others, the viewer's sense of narrative continuity is left undisturbed', as Jonathan Miller observes.[13] These film versions present the viewer with very different perspectives on the plays, and most significantly with something non-theatrical, in the sense of not being in the theatre, although some of these versions certainly owe a great deal to the theatre.

In the same way as it is possible to refer back to what we conjecture to have been the conditions of Shakespeare's theatre in our attempts to describe the relationship of audience to players and stage, and the influence this must have had on Shakespeare's theatrical discourse, so it is possible to refer back to the conditions for which individual films of Shakespeare's plays were produced. Before the advent of video cassettes, which we must remember are of very recent origin, no film-maker could have imagined his film being available for repeated showings in situations and at times chosen by individuals to suit themselves. Instead, film was made for showing in cinemas, to large gatherings of people, and in circumstances that, certainly in the Western world, the film-maker could more or less predict. He would know that it would be dark in the cinema, that there would be no other visual distractions, that people on the whole would remain silent, listening as well as watching, and that by and large they would remain for the whole of the performance. Most importantly, the audience would be experiencing the film in a communal way, individual responses to some extent conditioned by those of the whole group. Under these circumstances, it is instructive to inspect the overtly ideological purpose of Olivier's version of *Henry V*, which foregrounded Henry's kingly virtues, his heroism and patriotism and suppressed or distorted those scenes in the play which show other, less suitable qualities. The propaganda purpose behind the making of the film, and the conditions under which it was shot, operated as framing devices for the audience's experience, and the communal conditions under which it was shown, helped shape the emotional responses it received.

Shakespeare on television, made for television, also has a longer history than one might imagine, with short extracts and shortened versions of some of the plays already being shown by the BBC in the 1930s.[14] More recently, there have been the BBC Histories of the late 1950s and 1960s and other productions, leading up to the huge undertaking of the BBC Shakespeare, designed to show all the plays over a period of six years. What all these reproductions have in common is that they were conceived in televisual terms, and while techniques and the development of video recording have produced conditions of greater control over the editing and subsequent presentation of the version, nevertheless the particular constraints of the small screen affected the possibilities of reconstruction for all these performances. What also happened with the BBC Shakespeare was that it was intentionally produced to be shown and bought for innumerable reshowings on video. It is difficult to see what this did to the final results as seen on the small screen, in comparison, say, with productions not conceived in this way, but what it did to the conception of these productions will be discussed later.

Stage versions of Shakespeare which are either filmed or videoed undergo a metamorphosis in order to fit the different codes and conventions of the screen. In all instances spatial and physical relationships between the actors have to change, the relationship between actors and audience undergoes a transformation from one involving a common experience in a joint venture in the theatre to complete absence of audience on television, where the camera has to dictate what the viewer sees, in a way that does not happen with a stage performance, in spite of all the constraints to look in certain directions and at certain characters which a director can use on the stage. 'In the theatre the unattended part of the vista is still visible to the spectator so that peripheral events on the stage subliminally modify the experience of the salient ones' as Jonathan Miller points out,[15] whereas on the television screen the freedom and invitation to look elsewhere is non-existent. For example, in some stage productions the spectator is offered so much business to look at, undertaken by characters not actually speaking, that visual distraction from the main interlocutors is inevitable. With television, and film, only by not looking at the screen at all is it possible to avoid the visual coercion being exercised. Certainly, I would discriminate between versions of the plays on video which are conceived for television or video from the beginning and those which are intended to be relatively objective records of stage productions, such as the recordings now routinely produced by the RSC, which can be viewed at the Shakespeare Centre in Stratford. These are records for the archive, and are made by using four static cameras round the playing area, the tape then being edited to produce what looks like the best version for posterity. Even here, one must say, in many ways a new version is being produced, however objective the attempt merely to record.

To return to the consideration of what happens to a play in all these different representations, and of the differences between them: there is quite definitely a change of impact when a film is literally *reduced* to a video recording, or when a stage production of the play is video-taped. Some viewers who have seen the original stage version feel that the impact is less, that somehow the whole experience has been not merely changed but distorted and diminished. The unexpectedness of what a video text can present, as opposed to a stage reading, as opposed to the imaginative recreation of the study-based experience, results in much of the antipathy to television Shakespeare, quite apart from antipathy produced by critiques of the way in which television reconstructs the texts.

What happens to responses when a film is shown on video? What happens to the film itself? Does it become a different text? To the extent that the video viewer has the film under her own control, is likely to be looking at it either at eye level, or down on it, as opposed to looking up as in the cinema, one can see that the relationship between viewer and film is quite different. The dominance of the large screen, the larger-than-lifesize images, particularly close-ups, the powerful sound system and the fluidity and flexibility of camera use all contribute to a representation which engulfs and overwhelms the viewer in the cinema, and which is intended to do so. Conversely, the status of video as a powerful but nevertheless personally controllable part of the general living conditions of the viewer, which is seen surrounded by familiar objects, which can be, and often is, ignored while other more important things are dealt with within the domestic situation, makes the impact of the video less epic, less impressive.

At this point it is worth looking more closely at the BBC Shakespeare to analyse in greater detail what a deliberately designed video production is. When the BBC set up its project it was with the expressed purpose of making 'the plays in permanent form accessible to audiences throughout the world'.[16] The undertaking has provided teachers and students with the whole canon on the small screen. To make use of these productions in the classroom consideration needs to be given not just to the plays as they appear, or seem to appear, on the screen, but to the intentions and approach of each director and to the guiding principles by which the two producers, Cedric Messina and Jonathan Miller, were working. It is useful to have similar background information in relation to other Shakespeare videos, in much the same way as one seeks information about the intentions and interpretations behind a stage production (sometimes furnished in the programme). These BBC video versions were intended to have a long life, a permanence, and sales were expected all over the world, so what kind of cultural and economic interests lay behind this project? The project was funded by the BBC and by American money from Exxon, Metropolitan Life and the Morgan Guaranty Trust, and was initially in the hands of Cedric Messina as producer. Cedric Messina's aim was to produce the plays in what he called 'basic "classic" interpretations', an intention described by Gary F. Waller as 'naive':

> Messina's very terms, 'classic', 'basic', 'permanent', set up theoretical and, indeed, ideological barriers to the realisation of his other announced aim, to make the plays 'as vividly alive as it is possible for the production team to make them.'[17]

No discussion appeared to have been necessary about what these terms meant at the time, but underlying them seemed to have been the intention that an 'authentic' Shakespeare canon would be the result which would stand the test of time. When Jonathan Miller took over after two years, he recognized the impossibility of this position and indeed subverted it:

> I was limited . . . by certain contractual requirements which had been established before I came on the scene with the American sponsors: there are however all sorts of ways of skinning that kind of cat, and even with the requirement that I had to set things in so-called traditional costume, there were liberties which they could not foresee, and which I was able to take.[18]

So the original cultural objective, so impossible of achievement, but no doubt expressed in that particularly ingenuous way for the benefit of the sponsors, clearly was not fulfilled. In Jonathan Miller's opinion, it was not the commercial and economic basis of the series which damaged its cultural achievement, but 'many (other) things . . . not the least of which was its being on televison in the first place . . . Television forces you into a much more pictorial and scenic manner than I think is good for Shakespeare'.

The declared objectives emanating from the sponsors, implied here in Miller's account, are clear signs of the ways in which all these bodies see Shakespeare – of high cultural status, 'classic', 'traditional', and above all apolitical, part of the literary limbo to which all 'classic' writers are assigned in case they become politically and ideologically threatening. This is Shakespeare made safe. Graham Holderness describes the undertaking thus:

> The BBC/Time-Life Shakespeare series was produced in the image of the Corporation itself; a classical monument of national culture, an oppressive agency of cultural hegemony. The nature of the product itself inevitably acts to solidify the conservative tendencies of the institution, and to inhibit resistance from within. Hence possibilities for alternative or oppositional reproduction of Shakespeare must be sought outside the BBC.[19]

This is open to question, and there some critics who would argue that many of the productions show all sorts of disruptions, foregrounding and silences which can be used to open up the texts on the printed page as well as what is apparently being shown on the screen.

Holderness goes on to discuss other video versions, and other television approaches to Shakespeare, which appear to him to offer the kinds of alternative which he refers to above. In the meantime, the BBC versions provide a basic-fare Shakespeare which many teachers, and many pupils, will be using in the classroom. In many parts of the world where there is little opportunity for live theatre the BBC series provides the only possibilities for seeing Shakespeare in performance of any kind. This is particularly so in the USA, and indeed Tel-Ed Inc. backed up the financial support for the productions themselves with the offer of materials and workpacks to every secondary school, so that the American investment might be fully realized in pedagogical terms.[20]

Whether individual teachers see the productions as falling into the cultural pattern described above, or as providing material for study and comparison in the classroom, it remains important in my view that their pedagogic strategies include an awareness of these videos as constructed in particular ways, by directors who have particular views about the plays and about Shakespeare on television; some understanding of the ways in which television as an intimate, spatially flexible and all-powerful medium generally constructs its meanings; and some recognition that possibilities for radical challenge were by and large not used in the BBC series.

What connection does all this have with the classroom? To begin with, as I have shown in the discussion of the history of Media Studies, many English teachers have an antipathetic view of television and have done little to bring work on it into their classrooms. Because they are not skilled in the techniques of investigating and describing the way television operates, either in its construction or in its effect, they are forced to apply their literary critical skills when confronted by literature on television, or to apply the critical perceptions which they would bring to a theatre production. As the codes controlling any television production are not those operating in the theatre, nor those operating in relation to a deskbound study, these skills do not allow much analytical insight, beyond comparison with the printed text as used in the classroom, perceptions of where cuts and changes have been made, observations about the setting and the acting, and comparisons with theatre productions of the same play. What has not happened is any critique of the new-minted television text in terms of itself. It is at precisely this point that we hit the problem, for it is here that we face the crucial question: what are teachers using video versions of Shakespeare for?

I suggest that on the whole they are using them to enable students to learn the narrative sequences, to find 'character' illuminated by seeing and hearing the words of the play physicalized, to give the text some 'reality' and palpable existence, and so that students can visualize what up to then has existed only in their imaginations. But this is to attempt to treat the television text in the same way as the printed text has been treated, that is, from the standpoint that there is a reality which it is 'about', that it refers to transcendental truths and 'human values', that the play is a discrete entity, complete and whole unto itself, and that by reading, studying and then seeing the video of it we can somehow grasp that inherent meaning and confirm the intentions of the playwright. In short, the video version is used as an adjunct to a reading of the text, the next best thing to going to a live performance (although the differences between the two are noticed they are not used in analysis), and a way of helping students get to know some aspects of the text.

Three disservices are done by this: to the printed text itself, for reasons already discussed; to the television text; and to the students in the classroom. But if the radical critique for opening up the printed text is not available to more than a handful of teachers, what hope is there for a radical critique of the television text whether applied in the classroom or outside? The hegemonic nature of the cultural institutions in Britain, the powerful and successful means employed to disguise the constructed nature of television and other artefacts from the consumer – the viewer, spectator, or reader, the continual deflection of enquiry away from asking 'how', 'in whose interest' and 'who controls this' to generalized acceptance of what is presented as 'right and proper', the way things are and should be – all exert a fundamental influence on the way teachers approach work on television versions of the plays.

Students, too, have an experience of the text and of the video which needs some exploration. It has been said to me on more than one occasion that students have 'seen the video' of whatever play they might be going to work on, which implies either that there is only one video, or that it makes no difference which one is seen among different versions, because they are all essentially 'the play'. This reveals a great deal about what teachers are actually doing, and even more what students are receiving by way of messages about Shakespeare, or any other writer. When they have seen the 'video', teachers seem to expect that students will have some idea of the narrative of the play, and that they might possibly have understood something of the relationships established between the characters. Students when asked what they have understood from seeing the video reply with a range of responses, from 'didn't understand a word of it', to 'understood the story a bit'. Interestingly, little comment is made by teachers about the way the language of the plays comes across in the essentially 'naturalistic' medium of television, although this is the area of concern most often expressed by students. The fact that they don't understand the language on a first viewing, and comment on this, before they have read the play, means that however powerful TV is as a visual medium, the words used on it are at least as important, and as noticed.

If the video has been used in this way as an introduction to the play, and is often regarded by students as a way of avoiding 'work' for a lesson, it is rare for it to be used again once the play has been worked on in the classroom as a text. The video is used purely as a visual stimulus. If the video is used after the text has been read it tends to become a realism conferring agent, to the extent that students will say things like 'I didn't know he looked like that', or 'I thought she was older than that', thereby betraying their own subjection to the expectations of realism fostered by television, infinitely powerful in its conditioning of young viewers.

Unfortunately, unless we know how to undo some of this, how to help reveal to students that both the printed and the televisual text are constructed things, which can be made to say what you, or I, want them to say, and which are often used both on television and in the theatre to refuse fundamental confrontation in favour of the bland sentimentality of 'relevant to us now', we shall only compound the general tendency. My own view of using video in the classroom is that unless teachers are very skilled at the kind of deconstruction referred to here, have a grasp of the way television works, have the time to examine it closely, and are prepared to enable their students to make productive comparisons between printed and visual texts, then it is best avoided. I feel that using video is in many ways an opting out, seen by teachers as a panacea for the difficulties of having to deal with long texts with students who may not be very receptive to them. An inability to use those televisual texts in radical ways, along with a failure to understand the particular codes by which they are working, results in the whole unsatisfactory nature of the undertaking which is emphasized by the disillusion with Shakespeare exhibited by many students. Not one of the students I spoke to who had seen a video of Polanski's *Macbeth*,[21] for example, had enjoyed it, or even made very much of it.

To use these videos productively requires time and effort. Teachers must be prepared to use them in stages, to rewind and reinspect scenes or small parts to see what is happening, to have printed text available and to have already made that text a physical reality with pupils. I suspect that if collaborative, active, participatory work has been done on the texts, of the kind which I describe in Chapters 9 and 10, teachers will not feel quite the same need to use videos. Students will have made their own meanings with the text in ways that matter to them, and will not need to engage in the activity of making meaning with someone else's meaning-making of the text. In many ways, unless media studies is agreed to be the province of English departments – and, as I have shown above, this is hardly ever the case – then teachers do need to consider quite carefully why they need the prop of the video production in their teaching.

7 Race and gender in Shakespeare

In order to avoid collusion in the negative gender and race perspectives which appear to be operating in the Shakespeare texts (and it needs to be remembered that disregarding them is tantamount to agreeing with them), we need to be able to recognize these perspectives, to have our own strategies for confronting them, and some developed classroom practices for working on them. In other words, we require a theoretical base on which to build a workable classroom methodology. This theoretical understanding must work in two directions: it needs to be brought to bear on the texts themselves, and it needs to inform the direct relationships operating in the classroom between the teacher and the students, and among the students themselves. A discussion of these two factors must take account of their interrelatedness – it is, for example, pointless to recognize the racism in *Merchant of Venice* unless the teacher can also recognize the actual possibilities for race discrimination operating within the classroom and has a pedagogy for inspecting this with the students. I want to discuss the gender implications of the texts first, before moving on to racism later in the chapter.

The texts, whatever functions they performed for Shakespeare and his theatre in ideological terms, have been made to function for us as legitimators of particular constructions of women which have only recently been challenged. Along with all 'great' literature, the Shakespeare text has worked to confirm women in subordinate roles, defined sexually, socially and culturally by their individual men, and by the male-dominated social formation around them. This is not necessarily because the Shakespeare text intends such meanings, but because it has been made to yield them up in accordance with the ideological convenience of the times. Several feminist critics point out how editors and productions of the plays close off alternative perceptions of women characters other than those which fit the prevailing orthodoxy. For the nineteenth century, for example, this extract from George Brandes, the Danish literary critic, talking about Beatrice in *Much Ado*, aptly expresses typical responses:

> Beatrice is a great lady of the Renaissance in her early youth, overflowing with
> spirits and energy, brightly, defiantly virginal, inclined, in the wealth of her daring

wit, to a somewhat aggressive raillery, and capable of unabashed freedom of speech, astounding to our modern taste, but permitted by their education to the foremost women of that age.[1]

One senses some unease here, some discomfort with the kind of woman Beatrice seems to be, displaying such uncomfortable characteristics as aggression, which results on Brandes's part in some special pleading, following that emphasis on 'virginal'. If George Brandes could have been made aware of some of the sexual punning that Beatrice goes in for, he would have indeed been astounded.

For the twentieth century, certainly until the last twenty years, Brandes's Beatrice would have been perfectly recognizable. Indeed, this is still the preferred view of her for many people. But whereas the nineteenth century had no difficulty in accepting female submission, as with Kate and Petruchio in *The Taming of the Shrew*, to use another example, we now find that much more difficult to accept, and along with *The Merchant of Venice, The Taming of the Shrew* has become one of the problematical texts for our age. Contemporary directors face the challenge in different ways: in recent years there has been a production in which Kate submitted by indicating that both she and Petruchio knew that this was a kind of game, albeit a somewhat sour one (RSC, 1984), while in the 1990 RSC Tour production, Kate completely flabbergasted Petruchio, first by coming when he commanded, and second by saying what she did: he could not believe his ears. The effect of this was joyous and celebratory, with Kate's decision to play that part being more important than Petruchio's desire that she should submit.

These examples are indicative of the awareness that the plays can never be regarded as neutral, but perhaps also show that theatre companies faced with physicalizing and presenting the plays are probably rather further forward in this recognition, and the understanding necessary to do something about it, than teachers in schools. The key factor here seems to be *performance*. For teachers, usually not expecting to treat the plays through performance (although classroom 'acting out' may produce a similar challenge to conventional views of the plays) and often driven to a deskbound study of the text, other ways of seeing these texts do not present themselves. Through an active, investigative and deconstructive approach it is possible to recuperate other features of the texts, especially those relating to women. This approach is the basis of the work which I undertook in both junior and secondary schools which I describe in Chapters 9 and 10.

It might be useful here to look at what conventional views of the texts do present us with, before suggesting some ways of opposing them. For the particular constructions of women which a conventional reading would release we could investigate any one of the plays; the absence of significant women, as in some of the Histories, presents opportunities for investigation of a different but equally fruitful kind, the significance of absence among other things, both from the plays and from legitimated history. Obviously there are teachers who will already be treating the plays in this way, but the weight of editorial and critical opinion still favours a male-orientated, non-deconstructed evaluation. Any teacher faced with teaching Shakespeare and feeling uncertain about it, will find precious little mention of women in editorial prefaces or the critical references used in them which in any way challenges the status quo.

I referred to this situation in Chapter 3 in connection with *The Merchant of Venice*, for which the 1964 Penguin edition sported a preface which barely dealt with the Belmont scenes except in so far as they affected Bassanio. In similar fashion, the 1968 Penguin edition of *Much Ado About Nothing*[2] barely mentions Hero, although for obvious reasons it can hardly fail to mention Beatrice. Hero is 'bound to appear a little stupid' in a play which places such 'a high valuation on wit', and she and Claudio belong to 'the tradition of romance in which lovers endure misfortunes and tribulations before winning through to happiness at the end' and Hero conforms to the pattern in being 'the embodiment of innocence and simple beauty'. There are several observations I would want to challenge here, not least the reference to Hero's treatment at the hands of both Don John and Claudio, and then her father, as a 'misfortune' and a 'tribulation', and the implication that Claudio goes through the same degree of suffering. The view of Hero as 'a little stupid' exemplifies the difficulties of making very much of Hero according to this kind of critical stance; she appears to do little apart from occupying the victim's position and setting up a linguistically elaborate trick for Beatrice.[3]

There is nothing remarkable about this. As has been observed before,[4] editing Shakespeare is a firmly male domain. Women may be invited to provide the introduction to a new edition, as in the case of Ann Barton with the New Penguin *Tempest* and *Hamlet*, but they are rarely left in control of the Notes or Commentary. These are much more influential in shaping the understanding of the reader than the Introduction, which may well not be read at all and, moreover, has to contend with all the other criticism available for the particular text. Within this patriarchal set-up, which we must remember is as much to do with selling copies as with uncovering meaning, male perspectives tend to ensure that the critical attention is focused on the male world of the texts within which the women operate. The continuation of what might be called 'conventional readings' is guaranteed by this process. These readings result in a range of culturally and ideologically acceptable evaluations of the women in the plays, all of which ensure that women are returned to, or kept in, their 'rightful' place. Feminist critical readings of the plays have much to offer in place of this critical practice. In relation to the notion of women in their place, Kathleen McLuskie, in discussing the apparent mysogyny of the texts, suggests:

> A more complex discussion of the case would acknowledge that the issues of sex, sexuality, sexual relations and sexual division were areas of conflict of which the contradictions of writing about women were only one manifestation alongside the complexity of legislation and other forms of control of sex and the family.[5]

In other words, the conventional reading denies dimensions of significance in the texts themselves by ignoring the positions of investigation offered by the kind of historicism referred to by McLuskie. A conventional reading is, of course, one which reflects a currently dominant ideology; while the social formation remains essentially patriarchal, it is still the case that the male construction of women prevails and continues to be expressed in critical and editorial material. The George Brandes extract quoted earlier illustrates a rather differently focused view of women which fitted his ideological position in 1895. McLuskie's observation about forms of control of sex and the family helps throw light on the position of women in the texts both in a conventional reading and according to a feminist critique.

Conventional readings tend to work in the kinds of way I now propose to discuss, using examples from a range of texts. To begin with, women are defined and operate within the plays almost without exception in relation to men; that is, they are either someone's sister, niece, mother, wife, or future wife. They do not exist outside these relations, unless they are prostitutes, when of course their very 'profession' defines them in terms of male sexuality. This way of socially and textually positioning women is never challenged in conventional criticism, which can quite happily talk of Volumnia entirely in terms of her role as Coriolanus's mother, applying a range of critical approaches to him – psychological, among other things – in mitigation of what he does in the play, and constructing her as guilty and less than motherly. In case this should appear too obvious to warrant discussion, it is useful to apply this analysis the other way round, to men, and consider what a change in perspective would occur if they were viewed in the same way. The foregrounding of women, more easily done in performance than in the classroom, but still possible, reveals much about these assumptions. Where this kind of exercise proves impossible, because the feminine perspective simply is not there, an equally useful area of debate is opened up, concerning what the absence of women from the play indicates about its central concerns.

Where conventional readings cannot avoid seeing women as strong, and even central to the action, ways are nevertheless found of pushing them into the background. Lady Macbeth, according to G.K. Hunter, editor of the New Penguin edition,[6] provides the impulse for the murder of Duncan, but 'in no sense is this a shared action' in spite of her willingness to make it so. Macbeth's 'To know my deed 'twere best not know myself' is 'dialogue with himself', and Lady Macbeth remains 'accessory merely'. This partial reading ignores the balances in the scene, ignores Lady Macbeth's smearing of the grooms with blood:

My hands are of your colour; but I shame
To wear a heart so white

and ignores her own dialogue with herself before Macbeth appears, in which she recognizes her own nature:

Had he not resembled
My father as he slept, I had done't.

Lady Macbeth's death goes wholly unremarked in this introduction, as does her sleepwalking.

The structure of the plays in terms of the presence of women in them, their frequency of appearance, or lack of appearance altogether, is rarely remarked on. Nor have I come across mention of the fact that only one of the plays (*All's Well*) starts with a woman speaking, and only in two others (*Antony and Cleopatra* and *Much Ado*) does a woman appear on stage within the first thirty lines and speak. The lack of comment from critics about this indicates an agreement with the kind of status quo it implies, and also leaves uninvestigated the contextualization of women characters which has occurred in most cases before they appear on stage. By this I mean that even where there has been no mention of them beforehand, the patriarchal structure that has been established in the opening scene has already constructed our responses to them. Cleopatra is first mentioned, for example, in the language of denigration – while the words of Philo appear to be about Antony, they in fact apply to Cleopatra, who is the reason for his 'dotage', for his becoming a 'bellows and a fan to cool a gypsy's lust', for his having been transformed into a 'strumpet's fool'. For us this statement is pejorative in several respects, not least because the word 'gypsy' has racist connotations, which it probably did not have for Shakespeare. The statement can also be taken to be telling us something about Philo, but as his point of view is not of great import in the play, it is more to be regarded for the privileging of maleness which it expresses. Good masculine qualities like aggression are being vitiated by the sexuality of a woman. Having already been given a context for her which disparages her before she speaks, we then hear Cleopatra within the next lines undercut Philo's words by speaking of *love* and not prostitution. The conflicting aspects of Cleopatra which are offered in the rest of the play never quite overcome the negativity of this opening.

Conventional criticism does not question the roles women are seen in and expected to occupy in the texts. These include the complete compliance expected from daughters by their fathers, even dead ones; the passivity of many women characters who are on stage with nothing to say (what are they doing? watching the men?) even during scenes of great excitement and passion; their position/construction as objects, 'merchandise', goods, possessions, very often conflated with money or having 'value' which is expressed in monetary terms; their actions, seen wholly as the result of male actions, even though they appear at some points in the text to behave autonomously (for example, Juliet becomes the driving force behind the marriage to Romeo, but without his appearance at her family feast, deliberately looking for another woman, they would not have met – she was already being lined up by her parents for another man); the prerequisite of virginity in young women if their fathers are to marry them off successfully, and the speed and ease with which men, including fathers, can be made to suspect either infidelity or lack of chastity in their wives or daughters. The fact that this is rarely questioned or even mentioned by such critics indicates a condoning of that position and, perhaps more disturbingly, an inability to see that there is anything there to comment on; events in the plays are wholly driven by male desires, commands, jealousies and antagonisms, but again this is not commented upon, and indeed this stranglehold of concern is such that in some plays it is difficult to find an alternative, feminist way into it. Writing of *Measure for Measure*, Kathleen McLuskie says:

> Feminist criticism of this play is restricted to exposing its own exclusion from the text. It has no points of entry into it, for the dilemmas of the narrative and the sexuality under discussion are constructed in completely male terms – gelding and splaying hold no terror for women – and the women's role as the objects of exchange within that system of sexuality is not at issue, however much a feminist might want to draw attention to it.[7]

It is also very unlikely that this mode of analysis will deal at all with the material conditions operating in Shakespeare's theatre, which was an entertainment business working exclusively with men (shareholders, actors, writers and stage hands), and which therefore cast boys in women's parts, and for that reason kept the number of these parts down to five or fewer per script. This situation does not interest conventional criticism, except at the simple level of disguise convention, but does provide much food for thought for feminist critics. In a critical discussion of sexual difference in the texts, Catherine Belsey observes that

> the male disguise of these female heroines allows for plenty of dramatic ironies and double meanings, and thus offers the audience the pleasures of a knowingness which depends on a knowledge of sexual difference. But it can also be read as undermining that knowledge from time to time, calling it in question by indicating that it is possible, at least in fiction, to speak from a position which is not that of a full, unified, gendered subject. In other words, the plays can be read as posing at certain critical moments the simple, but in comedy unexpected, question, 'Who is speaking?'[8]

For the deskbound study of the text, which tends to produce readings of the plays as stories, the expressive realism of much criticism constructs these parts as wholly female, with all the concomitant expectations and description. The innuendo in what is said by a 'girl' dressed up as a 'boy', as with Viola/Caesario in *Twelfth Night*, is understood in that context, supported in current cultural forms by the cross-dressing characteristic of pantomime, and seen as 'saucy', possibly rather *risqué*, but essentially innocent. The dimension for sexual punning and *double entendre* afforded by a boy actor playing a female part in which 'she' dresses in boy's clothes, and, to continue using *Twelfth Night* as an example, then woos another boy playing a woman's part, on behalf of a man with whom she/he is in love, and who is her/himself loved by the boy/woman, is never seriously opened up for analysis. The plays are taken to refer to some anterior reality in which these women really are women, rather than constructions that exist not as literature, but as stage pieces. The realities for Shakespeare's audience would certainly have been the physical representation of women by boys, a dramatic language full of metaphor and punning which omitted no aspects of life as they knew and lived it, creating complexities of meaning and relatedness one strand of which was vividly and wittily sexual.

This last aspect of the texts is to be found only in critiques which have made it their central study, but which are rarely diffused into the mainstream of critical or editorial writing. Explanations for this state of affairs will vary, but it would seem that current ideology is attempting to hold a contradictory stance in place, and that sexual explicitness in relation to the Shakespeare text is still not part of the general system of acceptable discourses. Some of the meanings to be found in Shakespeare's punning would be found tasteless, crude and inappropriate by contemporary readers and audiences, yet exclusion of these meanings, and indeed ignorance that they exist, diminishes and prettifies the texts, reduces the possibilities for investigation, and prolongs a view of women in the texts which owes more to nineteenth-century constructions than to those of either Shakespeare's time or our own. We have still not fully outlived the silence about sex in literature, and the consequent hypocrisy, which we inherited from our Victorian forebears; this is hardly surprising, when we consider that our current ideology reflects and conditions a system of power relations based on a capitalist mode of production which is not so very different in essence from theirs, and which cannot disentangle its conflicting attitudes to women and to sexual activity since they lie at the very heart of its own contradictions.

The general silence about explicit sexual meanings in the texts, and about male and female sexuality as it surfaces in puns and references, means that many parts of the texts remain very difficult to explain and understand. Their meaning is in terms of sexual connotations, and the richness of meaning in relation to their context is completely missed under present circumstances. For example, the title of *Much Ado* is described by the editor of the New Penguin edition, R.A. Foakes, as in a tradition of 'deliberately puzzling' titles used in the 1590s which has 'of course a direct meaning in relation to the play's main action, concerning Claudio and Hero, which proves in the end to be ado about nothing'.[9] He also notes a pun on the words 'noting/nothing', and that is that. This seems to me to be deliberately obscurantist; even R.A. Foakes must know what 'nothing' can mean in Shakespeare, and by obliterating these meanings here does not explain the title. The word 'nothing' could also mean the female genitals, as the word 'ado' could also mean copulation. This extension of meaning in the title of the play indicates the suggestive nature of much of what is to follow, and allows us to see all the sexual relationships and suspicions being referred to in the title, making Benedick and Beatrice as important as Hero and Claudio. It tells us from the start that the play is about sex as much as about a fuss over trivialities. Similarly, the cherished notion of Hero as innocent, virginal, and therefore presumably ignorant of sex, is simply not borne out in the words she speaks. When she and Ursula are tricking Beatrice, they both speak words whose secondary meanings are sexual, and refer to any one of a great variety of sexual activities or orientations: 'disdainful', 'haggards', 'entirely', 'acquaint', 'affection', 'shape', 'rarely', 'fair-faced', 'ill-headed', 'winds', 'truth', 'virtue', 'fashions', 'press', 'death', 'wit', 'sighs', 'tickling', 'liking', 'excellent', 'angry'.[10] This confers on the scene a much greater depth than is produced by these innocent-sounding words shorn of their secondary meanings, and places the emphasis firmly on sexual coition, of one kind or another. We must not forget that in this play also, Beatrice, Hero and Ursula would have been played by boys, and their interactions and ambivalence generate these possibilities for ambiguity.

Students in the classroom, for whom these texts carry a particularly heavy cultural load, who may well be more critical and aware than many of their teachers of the gender implications of 'literature', are entitled to some kind of analysis of these texts in the ways implied in this chapter. Silence about these aspects of the texts is not good enough, although I recognize that investigation of the explicit sexual words and meanings may be impossible for many teachers. But investigation of the ways in which women appear in the texts, the meanings that we make now with those representations, comparison with current theatre productions, deconstruction of the texts or part of the texts, using methods some of which are discussed in Chapter 10, can all offer alternative meanings, and challenges to the current orthodoxy. Even if it is ultimately impossible to exonerate Goneril and Regan, for example, it is at least possible to see a *progression* into their ultimate positions, rather than assuming that they walk into the first scene already set on their course of action:

> A feminist reading of the text cannot simply assert the countervailing rights of Goneril and Regan, for to do so would simply reverse the emotional structures of the play, associating feminist ideology with atavistic selfishness and the monstrous assertion of individual wills. Feminism cannot simply take 'the woman's part' when the part has been so morally loaded and theatrically circumscribed.

McLuskie indicates here some of the difficulties encountered by feminist criticism in seeking other constructions of the plays, but difficulties does not mean impossibilities, and her subsequent statement holds out real possibilities for classroom study:

> Feminist criticism ... can be equally well served by making a text reveal the conditions in which a particular ideology of femininity functions and by both revealing and subverting the hold which such an ideology has for readers both female and male.[11]

Her concluding reference to male readers is especially important. In the classroom/study it is at least as vital that male students are encouraged to confront the gender issues at work in the texts, as that female students are empowered to challenge them. With the likely expansion of work on Shakespeare in school classrooms, we owe it to female students to indicate our own awareness of the male-gendered nature of most 'great' literature including Shakespeare, and to make Shakespeare no exception to any challenges we mount to this ideological position.

The position of female students in schools is itself the product of a whole range of constructions, generated and imposed through both the visible and the hidden curriculum, and owing much, of course, to powerful processes of coercion at work outside the school environment. In much the same way as it is possible to regard many of the significances of Shakespeare's women as hidden, so much of the potential for achievement, recognition and autonomy of female students is hidden, or deliberately obscured. Girls in mixed classes, for example, are very likely to be less willing to speak out or to contribute to so-called class discussion, to have significantly lower expectations about their future opportunities and careers, to have a more negative self-image, and to be more easily silenced than male students.

In these circumstances it is no more than to be expected that the reading matter produced for study will often reflect this bias and that texts used in class will reproduce the male as central. In some instances, particularly where a school or LEA has a working equal opportunities policy, and where there is a high awareness of these issues, this stereotypical description will not fit, and girls will find themselves and their concerns occupying centre place on a par with boys. Generally, however, and in spite of much of the effort made by educationists (and by some publishers anxious not to lose sales by not offering acceptable material), it appears to be the case that girls do not expect what is offered them to be much different in terms of its gender focus from what was offered to their mothers. The challenge, therefore, in relation to Shakespeare is to recuperate an alternative view from these texts, to make possible not only a change of perspective on the texts, but also a change of perspective for the students themselves. In Chapter 9 I discuss ways of ensuring that opportunities for boys to dominate are much fewer and that girls are given a voice in the process of opening up the text.

These same considerations of marginalization and subordination apply to black students in the classroom, especially where they are in a minority, and similar obligations to acknowledge their right to a voice and to recognition apply to the teacher in the classroom. Equally, the construction of characters in the texts as 'outsiders' reverberates in the consciousness of students and, as with negative gender perspectives, needs challenging. If, for example, Prospero's view of Caliban as a 'thing of darkness', and 'a born devil on whose nature/ Nurture can never stick' goes unchallenged, a whole range of discriminatory attitudes is being tacitly acquiesced in, as is the case with the Introduction to the New Penguin edition where Anne Righter (Barton) talks about 'Caliban's unalterable will to evil'.[12] If the white, male view exemplified by Prospero in this text is the only one allowed, both by editors, and by teachers in the classroom, how can students whose consciousness is based on other perspectives be enabled fully to participate in making meaning with the text?

It is more difficult to generalize about race in the plays than about gender. This is partly because the word 'race' in our contemporary usage does not exist in the plays; indeed, the word only appeared for the first time in English in the sixteenth century, so the range of meanings now attached to it was simply not available in the language at the time Shakespeare was writing. These meanings have gradually accrued since the early seventeenth century, in step with the systematic expansion of British and European economic power overseas. 'Racism' is the corollary of imperialism and colonialism – the racism which denies the humanity of its victims becomes a 'necessity' during periods of violent enslavement, conquest and expansion. This has been a feature as much of Nazi Germany in its treatment and destruction of Jewish and Soviet peoples in the twentieth century as of British treatment of the Irish in the nineteenth century; as much a feature of European brutality in the Americas from the sixteenth century onwards as of British brutality in the African slave trade from the eighteenth century onwards.

The Shakespeare texts do not show this fully-fledged dehumanizing treatment of others, but they do seem to show the first manifestations of racism as we currently understand the term. The treatment of Caliban, Othello and Shylock makes us uncomfortable and outraged, but we have more history to accommodate in our responses and have consciously attempted to educate ourselves out of the stock reactions to stock characters typical of one set of sixteenth-century discourses. However, it appears that while the Shakespeare texts work within certain conventions of stereotyping and stock characters, they also work to subvert them.

Plays which feature outsiders in subordinate roles, characters like Don Adriano in *Love's Labour's Lost*, Doctor Caius and Sir Hugh Evans in *The Merry Wives of Windsor*, Fluellen and Katherine in *Henry V*, can hardly be said to be operating in a racist way, but rather to be exploiting the potential for comic effect and misunderstanding to be made out of characters (whether stock or more complex) who do not speak English like the English, who use words inappropriately, and who behave in exaggerated and 'foreign' ways, and conversely out of the 'English' characters who do not understand or show themselves to be as linguistically incompetent. There are clearly many historical reasons to account for this treatment of outsiders and foreigners, many of which persist to this day, and many of which have contributed to racism as we know it. The texts, however, do not operate in one direction only: the gravedigger, for example, tells Hamlet that his madness will not be seen in him in England, where 'the men are as mad as he', and the French express a point of view of the English in *Henry V* which the text does not wholly disprove.

Each of the three commonly used texts featuring characters who can most appropriately be termed 'outsiders' (as opposed to 'black' or 'Jewish', for example) requires individual consideration and is engaged in a much more complex set of interactions with these characters. *The Merchant of Venice*, *The Tempest* and *Othello* undoubtedly share features of discourse in reference to these central characters, who are all outsiders. Their particular relationships with other dominant characters, compounded of oppression, exploitation and prejudice, differ quite markedly from text to text, while their construction as outsiders bears similarities. But even so, we recognize that Othello is not the same as Caliban, nor the same as Shylock. Othello, by virtue of the fact that he is the eponymous hero of his own play, and that he is a general in the Venetian army, is not equated in 'literary critical' terms with either Shylock or Caliban, nor is the treatment he overtly receives of the same order of viciousness as that meted out to those two. Othello is presented as the victim of one other person, and of his own inability to construe Iago's words for what they are, rather than as the victim of a whole social order.

The openings of these three plays, in the same way as other openings operate to frame our perceptions of women, contextualize these three characters before we see them. Shylock and Caliban are not mentioned at all in the opening scene of their plays, which is an indication of the other, equally important concerns of each text; the position of Shylock and Caliban in their texts is, of course, important, but not exclusively so. The opening of *The Merchant of Venice* contains a wide range of significances, some of which are not easy for us to grasp, conveying a multiplicity of meanings, many of them sexual. The focus of the play, as indicated here, is merchandise; the usage of the word slides between signifying cargoes on ships, portable property, and women and men as sexual objects in sexual and familial relationships with each other. We first see Shylock, therefore, only after the contextualizing of these first three scenes, and he then appears with no prior warning. His opening line of 'Three thousand ducats; well?' represents him instantly, but not yet prejudicially, as the supplier of the money promised to Bassanio by Antonio, rather than primarily in the role of 'Jew'. It is the case that within the context of Shakespeare's own theatre the mere appearance on stage of an actor representing a Jew, speaking those opening lines, would have triggered the expected and conventional hostile response towards Jews. But the interest and challenge of this particular text for us, lies in its own subversion of some of these anti-Semitic stances, and in the historically different perceptions and understandings which we bring to bear on it.

A different kind of introductory scene operates in *Othello*, and the development of its focuses through the rest of the play is complex. The opening scene involves two characters, one of whom, Iago, has already been constructed in the words of the other, Roderigo, as manipulative and untrustworthy. We tend to be wary of a character who has held someone else's purse 'as if the strings were' his, and when that same character explains why he does not love 'the Moor' we are alerted to expect only negatives from him. The play does not work in quite these straightforward ways, however. It is Roderigo who first uses the kind of crude words which we would now construe as racist – 'thick-lips' – and Iago who focuses instead on the sexual fears aroused by black males in white minds – 'an old black ram is tupping your white ewe'. The bestial references here, coupled with the further words they both use about Othello (Barbary horse, gross clasps, lascivious Moor) cast the so far unseen Othello in a sexual role whose description is characterized by its offensiveness, while the play simultaneously offers Othello's status as military commander as a counterweight. Before we see him we are oscillating between these two poles about what he is, and the rest of the play continues to work within this duality. The complexity of this play in relation to race and prejudice constantly destabilizes positions we thought we were safe in, about Othello both as sexual being and as a military man at the height of his powers.

In *The Tempest* Caliban occupies a role not shown in any other play, that is, the less than human creature; in Prospero's words 'a freckled whelp, hag-born, not honoured with human shape', a slave 'capable of all ill', a savage who did not know his 'own meaning' but who 'gabbled like a thing most brutish'. However, we do not meet this character until after Prospero, in charge of all the play's island narratives, has told some of the histories which precede the text, and after we have witnessed the terrifying and apparently death-dealing storm of the opening scene. Caliban appears within a context that has already minimized him, one that constantly seeks to contain and control him. He is, like Othello, a male with a potentially disruptive sexuality, a threat to the inviolability which Prospero has so far preserved in his daughter. His position as outsider has been brought about by the theft of his island from him, and by his subsequent enslavement by Prospero.

The fate of these three characters is similar: they have all been rendered impotent by the power structure in which they exist. Caliban decides that he will 'seek for grace'. The meaning of this phrase which is privileged in most editions and commentaries is that Caliban will seek for 'virtue', 'honour' and 'self-knowledge', that he will seek to become more like his white master, a fate which parallels the treatment of Shylock. Caliban has been rendered powerless, although we are left to speculate that he reinherits the island after the interlopers have gone home. Shylock has been reduced to nothing – he must turn Christian, waive half the amount Antonio owes him, and draw up a will leaving all his property to another Christian who from his point of view has stolen his daughter. His punishment and humiliation is then belittled by what follows: once Gratiano has had the last word about his wishing he could have been sent to the gallows, an overt and vicious racism which provides a frightening example of the irrational hatred engendered by prejudice, Shylock is completely forgotten, relegated to oblivion. By the end of the play he is merely the source of wealth for Lorenzo, and his daughter Jessica does not mention him again. Othello kills himself, performing the only act commensurate with the impossible position into which he has been manipulated and the appalling deed he has himself committed.

Each of these three characters has been made a fool of, has been reduced in stature, has been rendered incapable of participating in the prevailing power formation on equal terms, has seen the forms and manifestations of supremacy subtly shift and slide into unfamiliar and antagonistic shapes, and has ultimately been made into nothing. Like the women in the plays, whatever the force and strength of their initial position, these characters have been reconfirmed as subordinate by the end of the plays. What kind of messages does this transmit to students? And more importantly, how do we acknowledge and confront these features of the plays, while at the same time accepting the pleasure of the drama, and our own creation of meaning? One answer, rather than trying to construct an author behind the plays or to ferret out Shakespeare's intentions, would be to 'pay attention instead to the narrative, poetic and theatrical strategies which construct the plays' meanings and position the audience to understand their events from a particular point of view'.[13]

This statement offers suggestions for much deconstructive work on the texts, allowing students to understand how particular perceptions are produced in the reader or viewer, opening up possibilities for positing other focal points, other frames of reference, and challenging the traditional view of the plays from feminist or anti-stereotypical perspectives.

PART THREE

The classroom

8 Preparing for classroom Shakespeare

Much of what I have been arguing up to this point leads to the position which this chapter is going to address: that is, if previous critical and pedagogical practice has been so unsatisfactory for so many people on the receiving end of it, what are the alternatives? How can classroom experience of Shakespeare be made more enjoyable, more active, more challenging, more deconstructive? And can practical answers to these questions still cater to the demands of A-level or other examinations?

The suggestions which I want to make in answering these questions derive largely from a deconstructionist approach to the texts, and build on active and participatory ways of experiencing Shakespeare developed during the last five or so years, in particular by the 'Shakespeare in Schools' project which ran from 1986 to 1989. This chapter will discuss some preparation strategies and their underlying rationale, in fairly theoretical terms, while ways in which they were put into practice in primary and secondary classrooms are the concern of Chapters 9 and 10.

Many of the difficulties encountered by teachers and students in working on Shakespeare can be attributed to practising the 'head-on' tackle, which is determined to wring the 'meaning' out of the texts, word by painful word, line by painful line, in accordance with the meaning in the mind of the teacher, which has been acquired through a similarly painful process. Other approaches often attempted, particularly with younger pupils, involve a certain amount of story-telling of the narrative of the play, with some reading of the lines, a simplified version of the play, as it were, which excludes some complexities of plotting, and focuses on 'good' bits. The following anecdote from a Head of English in a Herefordshire comprehensive school illustrates just what can happen:

> The time had come to introduce 2B to the Bard. The trick played on Malvolio in *Twelfth Night* would be a good starting point. We read – or I planned we would read – a very simple narrative, interspersed with the noble Bardic words. I began . . .

'Olivia, a noble countess, mourned her brother ... Orsino, a noble duke, sent a messenger to woo her ... '

'Wot's that, Miss?'

'Wot a prat.'

'The disguised Viola, sent as a messenger, captured Olivia's heart.'

'Oo's this Viler?'

'Oliver must be thick if she thought Viler was a bloke, Miss.'

'Bet I could tell. Arf! Arf!'

We persevered. None of the girls could be persuaded to read, so, in true Shakespearean fashion, Matt read the part of Olivia.

'How now, Malovia.'

'No, Matt, Malvolio.'

'That's what I said: Malovio.'

'Repeat ... Mal'

'Mal'

'Vo'

'Vo'

'Lio'

'Lio'

'Malvolio'

'Malovio'

2B were fidgety by now so I abandoned my precision over names.

Craig, a specky child who read one word at a time, undertook Maria. We finished the story. Malvolio was let out of prison, and stamped off, threatening revenge.

'Nasty, inny, Miss?'

'Serve 'im right.'

'Don't you think he was punished too hard?' I enquired.

'Oo, no, Miss.'

'I could of thought of a better way.'

'So could I.'

'I would of ... '

I quickly changed the subject, promising a video tomorrow.

Tomorrow came, as it always does. 2B were sitting in an expectant circle.

'Wot we seeing, Miss?'

'The story from yesterday.'

'Great', came the sycophantic response.

'Miss, Jamie's head's in the way.'

'Shurrup you.'

'Oo's that with the yeller legs, Miss?'

The once delightful comedy now dragged out its length.

'Why do they talk funny, Miss?'

I abandoned my plans to let 2B act in little groups. In his encounter with 2B, Shakespeare lost 1-nil.[1]

This honest account shows very clearly the kind of experience with Shakespeare which many of us have had in the classroom both as pupils and teachers, but also indicates why it failed. The pupils were being asked to relate to a situation which was barely contextualized for them, which was about people whose actions seem incomprehensible, who used unfamiliar and 'funny' language, presented in a disjointed way through both simplified prose narration and the difficult language of the text itself. The experience not only of reading the text aloud like this, but of listening to it (what does one make of the girls in this class?) is unlikely to have imbued the pupils with a lasting desire for Shakespeare. The resort to using the video, which may have been a reward or may have been a bribe, is what many of us have done, but what is the real purpose of it? The pupils' response implies that it made little more sense than what they had already experienced, and bears out what I said in Chapter 6: video is no more capable than any other means of carving out a path straight to the transparent reality erroneously taken to exist behind the text.

The account also illustrates the fundamental need for preparation of a different kind: work on these texts, or even on the stories of the texts, is more likely to succeed by starting from a different position. Instead of the frontal attack, some creeping up from behind on the text and circumvention of pupils' resistances to the language is needed. The preparation that will allow a new approach has to be based on a new way of thinking about the texts; the kind of questions made available by a deconstructionist stance seem to offer the most fruitful and exciting possibilities as a starting point.

At its most basic level, one can describe a deconstructionist approach as one which seeks to take the text to pieces to see how it works. This highly simplistic definition is nevertheless useful because it enables the teacher to generate a series of questions about the particular text to be worked on, and also allows great freedom of manoeuvre: one can investigate how the text works from any one of a potentially limitless number of perspectives. I want to suggest some of the ways in which this investigative approach can be initiated, and the questions to bear in mind which can trigger it off. On a practical level, rereading the text before undertaking any work on it, however well you think you know it, is an absolute prerequisite. This is best done in one sitting, fairly quickly, with the focus on the general shape and structure of the text, rather than on specific details. This enables you to take an overview of the text, and to make decisions about where you want to start, and which parts of the text are most amenable to your purposes, and to the students who will be experiencing this with you. Some of the questions which I find useful in generating ideas for deconstructing chosen parts of the text can be listed as follows:

1 Who holds the power in the play? What is the economic basis of the play?
2 Is the power upheld/obeyed/challenged/overthrown?
3 What is the framework within which the play is operating, as indicated by its own internal evidence?
4 Is it possible to make *easy* judgements about the behaviour of any character?
5 How does gender work in the play?
6 How are women presented?

In the discussion of these questions and their implications for classroom work, I will refer to as wide a range of the texts as possible: these are the ones likely to be most familiar to teachers, from their own past study and teaching.

Who holds the power in the play? What is the economic basis of the play?

At first sight these do not seem obviously helpful questions and it is not immediately clear what they can reveal. But if we consider how power relationships and prerogatives define and control possibilities for action, and recognize that ruling groups always seek to maintain their power by whatever means are available to them at any given time, we can analyse some of the structures of power upon which many of the texts are built. Political, military and economic power is not expressed in Shakespeare as the kind of impersonal, Kafkaesque system unremittingly in control of individual lives, characteristic of the twentieth century: instead, the exercise of power is located very much in individual power-holders, whose actions are shown to affect not only those around them but themselves also. Readings of the plays focusing on this consideration indicate a society in perpetual tension, where control is always conditional, the individual exercise of power often corrupted into tyranny or irresponsibility, and benign patriarchy compromised into helplessness. Every text indicates in varying ways the structures of power on which it is based. The circumstances of the production and performance of some of the plays, which emerge from the shadows of the time, show how dangerously close to subversion some of the texts were treading. To display the way in which monarchical power is exercised, when the monarch in question can act immediately against you, is to be forced into the subterfuges of using foreign stories, set in other countries, and to be very careful to offer palliatives in plays about England, in the shape of extravagent praise of a historical monarch which can be construed as praise of the current title-holder.[2] Text after text shows power-holding called into question: in *Romeo and Juliet* a Prince who has connived for years at a murderous and pointless feud, who is so little regarded by his own citizens that they do not even stop fighting each other when he appears in the street, and who ultimately presides over the death of the innocent young; in *The Tempest*, a duke so naive in his exercise of power that he fails to see the threats to himself that his own self-absorption has created, but in turn using a different kind of power to take over an island from another being, and reinforcing that overlordship by physical violence; in *Julius Caesar* an overweening power-holder removed by violence, which unleashes more violence and more dangers; in *King Lear* a power-holder self-indulgently abdicating, creating the conditions for the disruption of all previous social agreements and the virtual destruction of the society. Even where the outward manifestation of power does not operate as a mainspring of action, some part of the story has always been predicated on social relationships as defined in terms of power.

The economic base indicated in the texts can similarly be opened up for inspection: land and money emerge as the determinants of economic status, and are referred to as palpable, physical realities, far removed from our contemporary complex relationships with unseen, untouched symbolic wealth and our almost total alienation from relationships with the land of the kind which formed the basis of much seventeenth-century economic power. Ownership of land confers power of the kind most sought after in *King Lear*, for example, motivating the children of the old men into barbarism to get it and keep it. Where money operates as the central pivot of a text, as in *The Merchant of Venice*, desire for it locks into every level of relationship, permeating not only the actuality of social and familial interactions but also the language in which they are expressed. In a more immediate way, dependence and power are often directly focused on actual coins and purses; in both *Othello* and *Twelfth Night* a weaker man is in thrall to a stronger, an emotional dependence signalled by a financial loss. Money and, to a lesser extent, land operate as the cash nexus, the beginnings of a system which defines human beings by their monetary value, and which is already valuing women in monetary terms.

Is the power upheld/obeyed/challenged/overthrown?

In many of the Shakespeare texts power-holding is shown to be vulnerable, unstable and constantly open to challenge. Where power appears to be secure from external threat it is often presented as unsure of itself, a prey to doubt and guilt from within. This inherent uncertainty transmits itself through into the surface words and actions of the text, so that even there we are constantly on shifting sands, endlessly seeking certainties which the text always denies. These dialectical features of the texts, manifested as contradictions, inconsistencies, silences and apparent irrelevancies, are the features least recognizable because they are the features most effaced and ignored in conventional treatments. The conditions of power-holding in the texts often go unremarked, even if not unnoticed, while attention is focused on the 'story' and the 'characters'. If, however, these features are foregrounded in preparatory thinking, the texts are made available for inspection of a different kind. Recognizing that no one is in the Forest of Arden out of choice, for example, but as the result of force, and knowing that they all return to the city at the first opportunity, offers new ways of looking at their behaviour in the forest, and at what they say about the forest. It also enables them to be analysed in terms of their relationships to power. What does it say about any of them that they were unable to resist the initial force? What does it show about their place in the society? King Duncan in *Macbeth*, however sainted and revered he is, holds power by proxy: the battle-ridden society depends on the military prowess of a Macbeth to survive. The king is shown to be not only weak but also naive: twice he trusts a thane of Cawdor, the second time fatally. Macbeth is shown exercising power at the other extreme, disastrously and increasingly tyrannically; neither Duncan nor Macbeth is satisfactory. The text *tells* us often of the 'goodness' of Duncan: but it *shows* us the inappropriateness of his kind of rule when faced with war and violence. The exigencies of *realpolitik* demand a mixture of political skills demonstrated by neither Macbeth nor Duncan. The most successful power-holders, like Henry V, offer dramatic proof of the validity of Machiavelli's contention in *The Prince* that 'a prince must know how to act according to the nature of both [beast and man] . . . he cannot survive otherwise.'[3]

The texts are full of statements about the nature of power and power-holding, each text embracing opposing perspectives, acknowledging the contradictions at the heart of all human affairs which also underlay the whole theatrical enterprise for which these texts were produced. The language of the texts similarly expresses these contradictions, through the equivocation, double meanings, puns and oxymorons in the lines spoken by most characters. This perspective on the texts allows the teacher to forget about the one 'meaning' of the text, and concentrate instead on ways of releasing the many meanings.

What is the framework within which the play is operating, as indicated by its own internal evidence?

This question is partly to do with the discourses at work in the texts and how these can be thought about to produce a viable classroom approach. The effect of the question is deliberately to isolate the text from any wider non-literary contextualizing and is almost an invitation to dehistoricize it. Given the difficulties of carrying out the necessary historical research, we can at least look at the texts for what they tell us about themselves. In some ways this information relates inexorably back to the previous two questions; thus the military/political framework in *Hamlet* could also be said to be about power. However, other considerations also operate, in particular the narratives of the text which constitute one of the main discourses at work. To the extent that every text is telling a story (an approach which lay at the heart of the RSC style of productions, where actors were encouraged to think that they were carrying the baton of the narrative, and must pass it on in such a way that the audience was enabled to grasp the story clearly), the ways in which the narrative works is extremely important. Sometimes it is intimately linked with power: Prospero, for example, controls many of the narratives in the play, and the ones he does not know, even though others in the play may know them (like why Claribel married the King of Tunis, and why the people of Argier did not put Sycorax to death), are left as tantalizing loose ends which are never tied up. *The Tempest* is quite different in this regard from, say, *Hamlet*. Whereas all the narratives are known to Prospero, no one in *Hamlet* knows more than 'is set down for him'. One way of dismantling the play is to look at what each character knows, about others, about events, about what is planned and plotted for the future. This narrative control may explain why *The Tempest* lacks the tensions and uncertainties, and therefore also the excitement, of earlier plays: in *Hamlet* it is never possible to feel that any one perspective is *the* correct one, even though some, like Hamlet's in his soliloquies, are privileged.

Examination of how these narrative strategies work is one way of 'undoing' the text, and also offers possibilities for further pursuit of the inconsistencies. It is common for these to be ignored, or to be plausibly explained away (usually by reference to Shakespeare having had his mind on something else, or an elusive pirate having mangled the text), but investigation of them confirms the plurality of meanings in the texts, and is also invaluable in showing how the reader works in relation to the text. *Romeo and Juliet* provides some good examples here. It is a text which places a lot of emphasis on time, constantly drawing attention to the time of day, the day of the week, years passing and how time appears to different people. Because narrative by its very nature is also concerned with time, and because a play on a stage appears to be presenting events in a sequential order, we come to expect a logical and proportionate use of time. But in this text time is clearly operating in all sorts of contradictory ways: Capulet talks of 'two more summers wither[ing] in their pride' before he will let Paris marry Juliet, and within a narrative day of this is insisting that they marry 'a' Thursday'. Juliet, after knowing Romeo for just over a day, has apparently had time to listen to the Nurse praise him 'above compare so many thousand times'. These apparent contradictions do not become obvious to the reader in initial readings, possibly because readers' expectations of 'realism' continually work to suppress inconsistencies. If for no other reason, it is important to use these features of the text to let students begin to accept their non-naturalistic nature.

The narratives are indicated in the opening scenes which hold the key to the rest of the text, and make clear the kind of story in which we are about to participate. This aspect of narrative discourse is another way of seeing how the text works: *King Lear* looks as though it could develop into a fairy or folk tale: the line-up of three sisters and an old father points in that direction. But maybe the uncertainty into which we are put by the very first lines of the play with that uneasy appearance of Edmund, has already alerted us to expect something different; the ways in which the text is different from our initial expectations are worth looking at. *Henry V* tells us, apparently, what it is going to be about, through the use of a chorus, as does *Romeo and Juliet*: but do we see what these chorus speeches promise?

Is it possible to make easy judgements about the behaviour of any character?

I ask this question on purpose to challenge the ideas that exist as part of the myths about the plays that particular fixed judgements are the 'correct' ones to make of characters. Similarly, I ask the question to ensure that stereotypical evaluations of characters, made easily available by much current commentary, but not so easily to be found in the texts, are avoided. Easy judgements and stereotypical judgements are closely related, of course, but there is a difference.

While an easy judgement on Cordelia is that she is 'good', it would be unlikely for her to be seen as a stereotypical good daughter, because she lacks the necessary meekness and humility. It is, however, common to find Shylock labelled as the stereotypical Jew, because he appears to exhibit the characteristics deemed to indicate Jewishness, and because of that to make pejorative judgements about his behaviour. Close inspection of the texts within the broad context afforded by an overview shows that neither of these judgements is borne out by the texts. Cordelia is only good if we agree that uncompromising honesty is good, if we agree that refusal to indulge the dotage of a loved father is good; the text is partly concerned to examine the results of this kind of inflexibility. This does not mean that Cordelia is 'bad' but that something rather more complex is going on than these simple labels would allow. Although the text itself privileges the idea of Cordelia's goodness, through the words of everyone who talks of her, except her sisters, the events of the play point in another direction; the deaths of Lear and herself appear to be part of the price to be paid for their initial rigidity. Shylock's insistence on his bond, which is rarely investigated for what it is in terms of law but mainly castigated for what it appears to be in terms of morality, is consistently denigrated within the text by other characters, and much of the text operates to convey a stereotypical view of him as Jew. However, the text also offers contradictory statements, from Shylock, about the experience of being Jewish in Venice. When he tells us that he has been spat upon, and kicked like a dog, that Antonio's interest-free lending of money is robbing him of a livelihood, whatever the effect of the rest of the text, we are brought up sharply against the daily reality for Shylock, and are invited to reconsider our initial view.

There is a large group of characters who are popularly regarded in stereotypical ways like this: Lady Macbeth who is wicked, the Weird Sisters who are also wicked, Goneril and Regan who are wicked, Caliban who is brutish and dangerous, Falstaff who is witty and jovial, Henry V who is heroic, Desdemona who is innocent, Hamlet who is a victim, and so on. For every action and statement which appears to justify one of these easy judgements, there is another which contradicts it. As I have shown with the examples of Cordelia and Shylock, the texts contain oppositional features. A useful line of enquiry with students is to investigate why it is so common for simple judgements to be the favoured ones, why it is so difficult to accommodate the idea of multiple and contradictory meanings in a text, when the discourses that surround them in their own lives continually offer plurality. Another useful line of enquiry is to ask why we, or they, accept these judgements so easily, and with so little questioning. What has conditioned us to be ready to accede to these stereotypes?

How does gender work in the play?

The idea of gender which I am referring to here is the complex and multi-faceted one produced by the shifting instabilities of personae and disguise. Chapter 7 was concerned mainly with gender issues as they relate to women and girls, and analysed some of the texts in some depth from that perspective. The wider issue behind this question is the notion of the instability of gender, and the relationship of that to the other unstable and contradictory features of the texts. Gender in these texts is signalled by a variety of means: names, relationships and clothing, and not infrequently by reference to features of behaviour and physique characteristic of men or women. The texts by themselves do not tell us that they were performed by all-male casts, so if we are limiting ourselves to what is available from the text on its own that consideration will be omitted. But before we do limit our perspective in this way it is useful to take account of the effect of this all-male casting on the language, innuendo and sexual punning of the texts, and on the limits which it clearly placed on certain aspects of relationships and interactions being shown on stage. Explanations of the sexual puns reveal that they apply equally to male–male as to female–male coupling, and the high rate of incidence of these puns indicates texts permeated with equivocal meanings, which refer to sexual activity of all kinds, in states of cleanliness of all kinds, between people of all kinds. Mostly we do not know or recognize these secondary meanings, although the level of energy and vitality they feed into the language of the texts is perceived by us as part of the 'richness' of Shakespeare.

If we return to looking at the texts in the ways we are most familiar with, the possibilities of sexual innuendo certainly exist in the texts which involve male/female disguise, involving references to homosexuality as well as heterosexuality: and homosexuality itself is evident in several relationships shown in the texts. It is still the case that this sexual orientation is rarely mentioned in any critical commentary, and even less often in editorial material, so that what is palpably there in the text is simply suppressed. It is fairly clear that the melancholy of Antonio in *The Merchant of Venice* is connected with Bassanio, and that the Antonio in *Twelfth Night* who risks his life for Sebastian does it from love. The Coriolanus–Aufidius relationship in *Coriolanus* indicates the same kind of male love, however compromised and compromising it is in relation to their military and political ambitions.

The key issue here is that we give recognition to the sliding about of gender identification in the texts, and that while male and female obviously exist as opposite poles of possibility, the uncertainties and confusions that exist between them are regarded as open to investigation. I gave the example in Chapter 7 from *Twelfth Night* of the disguise and cross-dressing involving the three central characters; other instances exist in *As You Like It*, in that agreement between Orlando and Rosalind that he will woo her as though she were Rosalind, believing her to be Ganymede, where allusions and remarks break through the apparently seamless surface of the text to indicate that he knows what he is doing and is quite happy to carry on. (Ganymede was, of course, not just the cupbearer of the gods, but a catamite, and the name was Elizabethan shorthand for homosexuality.) Teachers can go as far down that road as they feel comfortable with; it is usually the case in the classroom, for example, that it does not matter who is speaking any of the lines; students are quite happy to disregard that apparent male/female distinction, but further exploration of these features depends very much on individuals. It would be a very positive development for the recreation of Shakespeare in contemporary classrooms if the Victorian construction of Shakespeare which still exists in connection with the gender features of the texts could cease to be relevant for anyone and leave us to make new more appropriate meanings.

How are women presented?

Chapter 7 discussed at some length the issues which I consider important here, so the question is included here as a reminder of its existence. In my preparation of any text consideration needs to be given to how women are presented in order that both presence and absence can be investigated. As with men, they occupy a variety of social strata, in a variety of functions, and their supposed characteristics are used as part of the language of self-castigation of men: Hamlet talks of unpacking his heart like 'a very drab, a scullion/stallion', and at the end of the play is worried by 'a kind of gaingiving that would perhaps trouble a woman'; Lear prays against what he is already doing, 'let not women's weapons, water drops,/ Stain my man's cheeks'. The relationships in which women exist *vis-à-vis* the men in the texts vary, but love is always signalled by the man finding the woman beautiful, while the highest praise given to strong women is that they are like men: Macbeth exhorts Lady Macbeth to 'bring forth men-children only', a particularly ironic and disturbing wish given that to reach this pitch of steeliness she has unsexed herself, and made child-bearing metaphorically impossible. The closeness of much of what is to be revealed by looking at women in the texts to what I have said about gender is self-evident.

Classroom practice

Some indications of how these preparatory thoughts and investigations can result in classroom practice follow. A useful guiding principle is to be convinced that the text is not sacrosanct: you can do what you like with it. Use parts of a scene, use single speeches, put two speeches together, give pupils individual lines to speak, cut the scenes down to their skeletons, focus on dramatis personae who do not have much to say and consider events from their perspective, break the text up and look at bits from different places in the play side by side, develop non-speaking parts, substitute boys for girls and girls for boys. If you are looking at power in a play find a way of making this concrete for the students – turn Lear's handing over of everything into a game of swap, where cards with the appropriate words on them are exchanged between the king and his daughters, and ask the pupils who has now got what, who has the power. Turn the casket scene in *The Merchant of Venice* into a guessing game, where pupils have to attribute the correct couplet to each casket, and devise their own set of contents for the losing and winning ones; use any of the methods advocated by the 'Shakespeare in Schools' project, or those usefully listed in Appendix 6 of the Cox Report, which can be applied to a Shakespeare text as much as to a novel. The suggestions are obviously endless.

Pedagogical principles which ideally underlie all approaches to work on the texts are listed here:

1 It is very important not only to make sure that each pupil is participating, but that all pupils know that their contributions are valued, and will be asked for.

2 It is very difficult to achieve anything approaching this if pupils are sitting in desks facing the front. The power relations in the class operate too strongly, and produce undesirable behaviour in the pupils, that is, those who are prepared to speak out are left to make the running by the others, who either have a rest or opt out mentally.

3 A circle of chairs is one good way of redistributing the relationships in the class, and of placing everyone, including the teacher, on the same level.

4 It is much more evident to pupils sitting in a circle that each one of them is valued equally if they are each in turn invited to contribute in one way or another, and are therefore also being expected to *listen to each other*.

5 This arrangement also enables the teacher to make sure that the boys do not dominate the class, as they mostly do in conventionally arranged classrooms. Not only that, but because they attempt to dominate, they attract an unfair share of the teacher's attention, which perpetuates the girls in their roles as 'quiet' and 'well behaved' and lets them off the hook of being expected to contribute.

6 This arrangement also ensures that pupils who normally might feel that they were 'thick' (to use a term by which pupils often describe themselves and others) or pupils who feel insecure for other reasons, can feel recognized. Even if they are unable to respond when it is their turn (and they should not be forced into speaking), they should be given the opportunity to come back later with their ideas.

7 Work on the texts should be devised to make no distinctions between pupils on any grounds. The guiding principle in preparation should always be active participation. It is always best to find an active way into working on the texts, and sometimes it is best not to do anything at all if an active approach cannot be found.

8 The language experiences offered by the Shakespeare text are challenging but rewarding, so the more pupils can be required to say the words, the better. Gradually pupils realize that the words are far less daunting than they seemed to be at first, and they begin to savour and enjoy the language.

9 The key word to bear in mind is *involvement*. If pupils are involved they are likely to enjoy, and if they enjoy what they are doing they are likely to learn. At the same time the *entitlement* of the National Curriculum philosophy is an informing idea behind the preparation, and the injunction that pupils experience some of the works of Shakespeare is being carried out.

10 An important pedagogical consideration is to ensure that no pupil is exposed and made to feel vulnerable in front of the class. This leads to an emphasis on

group work, collaborative work of all kinds, and avoidance of 'performance' or 'showing' by the pupils unless they are all engaged in them.

11 The work which produces the best results depends for its effectiveness on a shared and sharing attitude, a communal sense of purpose and commitment, and a willingness to do all that is asked: the teacher must, therefore, not ask for more than pupils are able to give, but similarly must be wary of asking for less.

12 The establishment of an atmosphere of purposeful engagement at the beginning of each lesson is best done by a communal drama activity, even if it is only simple warming up and concentration exercises. Ten minutes of introductory drama work is all that is needed but it serves to establish the rules and expectations of the teacher during the session, and helps pupils ditch all the distracting emotional baggage they have brought with them into the classroom.

9 Shakespeare in the primary classroom

I will present this chapter as an ongoing account, written in the present tense. This will much better convey the immediacy of the situation, and the challenges that arose throughout the work. I was working for a term or so with two primary school classes, in the same school, which were vertically grouped and consisted of pupils aged 9, 10 and 11 years (years 4, 5 and 6 in the new nomenclature). The teachers were very enthusiastic, one particularly so because she had been a secondary school teacher of English who had retrained for primary teaching. Her secondary training and experience meant that she knew some Shakespeare. It was her idea that we should work on *Macbeth*, which she knew well. The pupils all lived locally in a depressed urban environment, characterized by mixed housing and light industry, and were at very disparate levels of reading and writing. Both teachers thought the pupils were the most difficult classes they had ever taught, with individual exceptions.

After an initial meeting to discuss possibilities, and a second more detailed planning meeting, I arrive for the first lesson. It has been agreed that I will come in every Wednesday afternoon, and work with each class in turn, so the work will be spread out and will need to be developmental. I am committed to making it enjoyable and active for the pupils, and to ensuring that as far as possible they are all involved all the time. The strategy I am going to use is aimed in two directions. The first is to ensure that the pupils have a clear grasp of the narrative line, and the second is that they use as much of Shakespeare's language as possible, and are up on their feet, actively participating.

I decide to start working on a kind of problem-solving exercise, where I ask the class to come up with ideas about who might own a crown, a sword and a cauldron. After discussing this in their groups (they are at 'tables' in the classroom) all pupils contribute enthusiastically, and ideas are listed on the board for all to see. They contribute predictable ideas about the crown and the cauldron, but are more surprising about the sword, suggesting both 'good' and 'bad' people, unconsciously expressing the literal and metaphorical double-edged nature of both the sword and Macbeth. I ask them to choose one person from each list for their own story, and later they will write a story which is about the three people they have chosen. To round off this session, I give them lists of words taken from *Macbeth* which are used in the text about the King, Macbeth and the Weird Sisters. I ask them to decide which words go with which characters, and we make a new list on the board. I decide that this is only partly a good idea: it allows them to experience words they have probably not heard before, and to put them in their own context, but I doubt if they will be able to use them actively yet. The session ends with the pupils very keen to write these stories.

In the second session we read the stories together, in as active a way as I can think of. First, pupils on each table read each other's, and then decide which stories should be read out loud to the whole class, and who should read them. This may not have much to do with Shakespeare, but it has a lot to do with other aspects of this teaching that I am just as concerned with: that is, to help pupils recognize each other's contribution, and to allow the least confident to be able to speak out. It's a group development exercise. The stories are read out, sometimes by the author, sometimes by me, and the listeners are asked to give marks out of 10. I don't really like the idea of marks, but it gets them listening, and they are very generous anyway, so I don't feel I've compromised my philosophy. They are learning very quickly how to listen, or at least to be quiet, and not to call out or interrupt. There's a good communal atmosphere in the classroom. The pupils really enjoy the whole of this work. Now I feel I'm beginning to get to know them, and to recognize pupils I shall have to keep an eye on, to make sure they can participate in what is to come.

In the third session we are going to use Act I, scene 1 of the text, and we are able to use the hall. We cannot sit in a circle of chairs because there are none, so for all this work we sit on the floor or stand. The pupils in the first group are very excited and likely to run a bit wild, so we have to do some concentration exercises to calm them down. We play a game called 'Jack to Jill', which involves crossing the circle to a named person while calling out your own name: thus John crosses the circle to Karen, saying 'John to Karen', and then Karen must immediately cross to someone else, using the same formula. It is usually used to help people get to know one another, but I use it here for concentration, and after one round I speed it up, so the pupils are running across the circle. I could have used other exercises, but this one seemed most appropriate. We then do a listening exercise where they are asked to listen for sounds outside the room, and then inside the room, keeping silent themselves. This is all a little hurried, but it seems to work. We then start looking at the scene.

With the other group, the level of excitement is so high that I quickly improvise a calming exercise to quiet them down. They all lie down on the floor, in a comfortable position, close their eyes, and listen. This takes some time, there are always a few pupils who find this difficult, but eventually we are all quiet, and then I start telling them about the place where they are in their imaginations. I attempt to evoke the heath, doing a 'realization' of the opening scene in words, so I talk of the darkness coming on, the mist and fog, the sounds of battle in the distance – swords clashing against swords, horses neighing, and so on – all the time talking to the pupils as though they themselves were there walking through the landscape. To bring us to the scene of the text, I tell them that they see three strange shapes on this heath, which they cannot recognize – are they human or are they something else? The strange shapes move and stand up, and then they see that they look like women, and have skinny lips and choppy fingers and their clothes are withered and wild. At this stage I have to get them out of the trance I have tried to induce in them, and tell them that they have got so close to the figures that they must open their eyes and sit up. Both these introductory approaches seem to work well with the particular group, and both bring us to the point of using the text, which has already been photocopied and enlarged, one sheet for each pupil. We are now in a quite different kind of interaction, where reading becomes important.

I get the pupils back in a circle sitting on the floor, and give out the photocopies of Act I, scene 1. Then I go round the circle allocating one line to each pupil, starting again at the beginning when I have run out of lines, so that the lines will be spoken at least twice each. Each pupil now has a line to say, and we go round the circle in turn practising the lines. Some of them find their line a bit difficult, but manage to say it with help from me or their teacher. We go round the circle again, saying our line each. Then we go round the circle again; pupils walking in turn to the centre of the circle to say their line and then going back to their place. Some of them are rather quiet, so we do it again, shouting. By now, they have heard the scene four times, and are beginning to get the gist of it. I ask them to say what they think is happening, and they can answer all my questions about what is going on, and who the Weird Sisters are waiting for, and what the weather is like. Now, I ask them to learn their line, and we go round the circle again, saying lines without looking at the sheet. This presents great difficulties to some of the pupils, who have never been asked to learn anything by heart before, and who find their lines a bit of a tongue twister. However, they persevere. I ask them to play Jack to Jill again, but this time they just say their own line as they cross the circle to someone else. This is done with great enthusiasm, and much laughter, but everyone (nearly) gets their line right and feels proud of what they have done. We then go round the circle again, passing lines on from person to person, so the first speaker addresses their line to the person on their left, who then turns to the person on their left to tell them their own line and so on: it is like a chain of communication and makes them look at each other as they speak. We finish the lesson by joining hands in the big circle, and moving round together in rhythm with the lines, saying them all together as we go. We do this twice to make it more fun, going faster and faster. I feel quite pleased with this lesson, and am really gratified to see that even the weakest pupils managed to learn their lines, and that they were joining in with the rest at the end. I also feel pleased that the lines have been physicalized for the pupils who have begun to experience the relationship between the iambic pentameter and their own movement.

Their teacher is surprised at how well they have managed, and is particularly pleased at their commitment. She says she will get them to write something of their own about witches, before I see them again. When I arrive for the next session, the pupils are clamouring to show me their work, and David comes up to me to tell me his line from last week which he had found hard, and announces in a loud and confident voice, 'In thunder, lightning or in rain', and then grins proudly. I am full of praise for this achievement. David continues to quote this line at me for weeks afterwards. This is what two of them wrote:

There were three witches
On the heath
Talking
in a *spooky*
Language
What do they talk about
Where to meet
In thunder or rain
To meet Macbeth
And Grey Malkin
We shall meet
Before the set of sun
When the hurly burlys done
When Paddock calls.

Three Witches
Upon the heath
And the cat Grey Malkin
One witch had warts
One had teeth black as night
The sky was filled
With fear and fright
Nobody would come out at night.
Thunder hail and lightning
Is frightening
In the cauldron
Water boiling
Witches singing
Spells out loud.

In this session we are going to do some work on the battle and on the Weird Sisters meeting Macbeth. We could dramatize this but I have decided to stay in the classroom for now, to let them become familiar with the witches' words, and to tell them some of the story. I am using the Captain's speech from Act I, scene 2 to give me the narrative line for the battle, and then I am going to tell of the witches meeting Macbeth using some of their words from the text. The class teacher is at the board, chalk at the ready, for when these words need writing down. I tell them about a bloody battle, fought with heavy two-handed swords that the pupils would hardly be able to lift, of how tired and filthy the soldiers become, how dismal the weather, how they can't see each other in the fog, and so on. I involve the pupils with this story-telling as much as possible, asking them to guess, to give their own ideas, to mime a two-handed sword. When we get to Macbeth unseaming MacDonwald 'from the nave to the chops' and fixing his head 'upon our battlements' I ask for a volunteer to demonstrate it on, and the class are all suitably revolted, except for the swaggering boys who think it's good.

Now is the time to remind them of the witches. What were they waiting for? Macbeth. Where are they? On the heath. Where is Macbeth? In the battle. When the battle is over, and his side has won, what will he do? Go home. Where? Across the heath. Who will meet him? The witches! Why do they want him? At this stage all suggestions are welcome, and the pupils come up with quite a lot of good ideas, until one boy who has been thinking quietly suggests that they might want to tell Macbeth something about him being the king, something to do with the crown. I am inwardly delighted to hear this, and agree that this is indeed what the witches want. The question is, what do they say to him? They are all agog to hear what is going to happen. A bit more description is required here ... Macbeth is tired but pleased, and walks across the heath with his friend Banquo, when out of the mist appear three figures. The men do not know what to make of them, do not know whether they are male or female because they have beards but otherwise look like women. Suddenly the first witch cries out to Macbeth: 'All hail, Macbeth! Hail to thee, Thane of Glamis!' I explain what a thane is and ask the pupils what Macbeth thinks when such a strange figure whom he does not know greets him by name out on the wild heath. They think he'd be rather surprised and maybe a bit frightened; disagreement here, he wouldn't be frightened, he's a brave soldier, yes he would, he's never seen them before. Then the second witch greets him with the words, 'All hail, Macbeth! Hail to thee, Thane of Cawdor!' I explain that there already is a Thane of Cawdor. What does Macbeth think now? How can he be Thane of Cawdor when there is one? What do the witches know that Macbeth does not? Lots of suggestions here, including the idea that if they know magic they might know that the Thane of Cawdor is going to die. Just to keep the suspense going, I ask the pupils what they think the third witch is going to say to Macbeth; lots of guesses, including one quite near the mark, so I tell them: 'All hail, Macbeth, that shalt be king hereafter!' Their teacher has been busy writing these lines on the board, so we can all read them out together now which we do. We take a break while the pupils write the lines in their books ready for later reference, and then discuss what Macbeth might be thinking now. How can the witches be right? Does he believe them? How could it come true? Lots more ideas and offerings, from most of the class, until one of the boys says: 'They might somehow get him to kill the king, not do it themselves, but make him do it.'

The rest of the class think this sounds like a sensible idea. I tell them that not long after the witches had spoken to Macbeth, a messenger came to announce that the Thane of Cawdor had been executed for treason. Much excitement! What will Macbeth think now? We finish the session with my telling them that Macbeth has a wife at home who is called Lady Macbeth, and that he writes a letter to her telling her about what has happened. Their teacher says they will do that before I come next time. This is what one of them wrote:

My darling Wife,
     It wont be long till I come back home to the castle and see you again. I hope you have been keeping yourself busy whilst I have been away.
     Lots of things have been happening here. As you know I was on King Duncan's side and we were fighting Mighty Macdonald and his army. Well, guess who won? Macdonald is no longer mighty! I took my sword, held him from the hair and unseamed him from his nave to his chops. Then I stuck his head dripping with blood and gore onto a spike on the top of the battlements. It was a grand sight. I wish you could have been here to see it too.
     To celebrate my victory I went for a walk on the heath with my friend, and to my astonishment I encountered three of the strangest creatures I have ever seen. At first sight they looked like old ladies – a bit like Maggie, your lady-in-waiting – but when I approached I could see that they had ugly faces covered in pimples, straggly beards and bent fingers with long pointed nails. It was ghastly – my hair stood on end!
     The first creature spoke to me, 'Hail Macbeth thane of Glamis'. Well how did it know my name? Then the second one made a remark and said: 'Hail Macbeth thane of Cawdor.' But as you know this is not true. However, the best is yet to come. The very next morning, Ross the messenger delivered a letter proclaiming that the thane of Cawdor was a traitor to the king and had been executed and I was to be made thane of Cawdor! Now if that prophecy has come true, wait till I tell you what the third ugly creature told me. It said: 'Hail Macbeth that shalt be king hereafter.'
     What do you think of that my beloved?
     We shall have to wait and see if it comes true.
          So farewell my love until we meet again.
               Macbeth.

The pupils are very taken with the idea of unseaming someone from the nave to the chops and later in the term their teacher tells me of a supply teacher who had been with the class and found some of them very difficult to handle. In desperation she turned to one of the quieter ones and asked him what their proper teacher did to keep them under control. He answered, 'Oh, she says she'll unseam us from the nave to the chops if we're naughty'. Supply teacher totters into staffroom at the end of the day saying, 'Not only are they the worst class I've had to look after, they quote Shakespeare at me!'

     With one group at the next session we work on the Captain's speech in some detail. After a short warm-up, I tell them that I want them to repeat the words I say, and do an action to show what the words mean, so, for example, when I say 'Doubtful it stood' they might shrug their shoulders, or some such gesture indicating doubt, and so on. We start. The Captain's speech is full of vigorous and energetic words and ideas, and they grasp what I mean quite well. The repetition is more difficult for some of them, but I egg them on, and when they speak too quietly I shout out 'What?' or 'Two spent swimmers did *what?*' and make them shout the words themselves. Their movements become more energetic and more accurate, and they use each other for the two spent swimmers and for the death of MacDonwald. I then give them a phrase or a line each to say from the speech and a photocopied sheet of it, and having now heard the words several times, they are fairly confident with their own bit. We try it round the group and then I ask them to go to one end of the hall and run across the hall in turn shouting out their line as they go. This really energizes the words, and they think it is most enjoyable, and tell me their lines the following week, too. Back in the classroom in the same session I tell them that the king has decided to visit Macbeth and Lady Macbeth at home, and that the castle will need to be prepared for the visit. They are invited to decide who would be working in the castle as servants, and they make good suggestions. Each person who makes an acceptable suggestion becomes the organizer for that particular job, and then chooses staff from the rest of the class. This allows me to give some responsibility to some of the pupils who find difficulties, and they take their duties quite seriously. This development is left for the next session.

During the next session with the group we mime and act out the whole sequence of preparing the castle for the king's visit, the arrival at the draw-bridge, the guards escorting him in, the evening meal, and the king and his entourage going to bed. This does not work as well as I would like, because the pupils are not used to that kind of freedom and become rather silly, so I realize that much tighter preparation is needed, and that they cannot handle this kind of 'acting out'. I realize that I should have known better, but decide to refine the idea for another time.

With the other group, we go straight on to work on Act II, scene 2, where Macbeth murders the king. To get us to this point of the story, I tell them about the king's decision to visit Macbeth, and about the castle being prepared, and invite their own ideas and suggestions to incorporate into the narrative. The work I have prepared on the scene has already worked very well in another junior school, so I hope it will work here. It is designed to get them to read some of the words of the scene, to work out sequence, to guess what might be happening, and to make sense of what they are given. They are put into groups of three pupils. Each group is given 30 cards with 30 lines from the scene, some spoken by Lady Macbeth, some by Macbeth. The speakers are not indicated on the cards. The lines have been chosen to offer the bare bones of the scene, the essence of what is happening. The groups read out their cards to one another, trying to work out what they are about. I give them about ten minutes, and their teacher and I circulate round the room, giving help where needed, but not giving any answers. Then we stop, and I ask if anyone can tell us what seems to be going on in the scene. Someone's being killed. How do you know, what gave you that idea? Because it says here something about daggers. Read out the card, so we can all hear the words. 'Why did you bring these daggers from the place? They must lie there.' Can you tell us anything else? And so on.

By dint of these kinds of question, and pupils reading out from the cards the words that support what they are saying, they gradually build up the picture of what is happening in the scene, and become more and more excited as they realize that the person being killed must be the king, and that Macbeth is killing him, and that both Macbeth and Lady Macbeth are terrified. Why didn't Lady Macbeth kill the king? Why won't Macbeth take the daggers back? When is all this happening? How do you know? Prove it, prove it! Read out the words. I insist that they read out the words, and even the poor readers are so keen to prove what they've realized that they too read out, somewhat clumsily, what is on their cards. (When I used this in the previous school, the pupils (who were 10-year-olds) remembered the words and could quote them back at me three weeks later after the Christmas holiday. A supply teacher who was with me as we did that work was absolutely astonished that these pupils could cope with and understand the words. At the time I thought that this said a lot about teachers underestimating pupils, and about teachers expecting Shakespeare to be incomprehensible.)

In the next session we work on the same scene, but we are in the hall and we are going to make it very physical. Their teacher asks if we could do something with all the work so far to turn it into a presentation for a performance evening at the local comprehensive school, and this gives an added impetus to the work. We form the circle again, and each pupil is given a copy of the scene and allocated a line or phrase, as before, but we are going to use the whole scene this time. There are more lines than pupils, so they are allocated two bits each. First we try round the circle in turn, saying our lines, to get the feel of them. Then we try again, seeing what happens if we whisper them, and then what happens if we shout them. I ask the pupils which they think is the best way. They think the whispering, and I ask them why. They say it is because it is a creepy scene and it's all about a murder. Then we try another way of doing the scene: with sound effects provided by the pupils, who really have to be alert as we read round because they still have their own line to do as well as the sound effect they volunteered for. The scene is full of noises: the owl, the cricket, the bell, the voices calling out in sleep, the knocking, so there are lots of opportunities for really acute listening, picking up of cues, and voice control. We have not worked on any of these things in any depth, and the first time we try the scene like this there are lots of pauses while pupils find their place in the script and lots of nudging and urging from other pupils to the laggards, but we all feel some of the urgency of the scene, so we try again and this time it goes really well.

To prepare the scene for the performance at the comprehensive school, I divide the class up into a group of sound effects pupils, a group of readers, and a group of mime actors. We practise each group together to get the continuity, and the sound effects group have the most difficult job because they must be very alert for their cues. They manage it really well, making sounds which they work out for themselves, really weird and other-worldly. One girl brings her portable keyboard and produces some introductory sounds/music for the performance, and some more for the other bits we perform. The readers, six pupils, are going to read the scene in the way we've been doing it up to now, to keep the disembodied effect of many different voices reading, which allows attention to be focused on the two main actors. We have a Lady Macbeth and a Macbeth, who are to mime to the words, so we have to designate parts of the hall as the bedchamber, the lower room where Lady Macbeth is, and the landing where the grooms are (or are they to be imagined in the bedchamber? I see that this is an example of my own tendency to want to visualize the events in a 'real' setting – I realize that once you start actualizing or performing a scene, you are bound to think of physical space in certain ways, and that for children it seems necessary to make it as concrete as possible. However, I also remember children's ability to turn any space and any object into whatever thay want it to be.) Between sessions the pupils do some writing in response to the work. Two of them wrote like this:

My heart was beating fast
Until at last,
I did it – the deed was done.
His last, laboured breath
A sign of his death.
My hands were filthy,
My mind was guilty,
Blood everywhere.
I can't go back there.
A bloody sight.
A sorry sight.

The deed is done
The battle is won
The king is dead in his bed
Macbeth came walking
Down the stairs
Blood on his hands
As red as sun
At sunset
The dream will hurt
The king bleeding
Smear blood on the grooms
Wipe the sorry sight
From his hands.

What happens finally after we have really rehearsed is that the king lies down in the bedchamber, on the floor, the sleepy grooms drink their possets and fall asleep immediately in strange positions near him, the sound effects team are all in place at one end of the hall, and the readers are in position at one side of the

hall. Lady Macbeth walks in and at the same time Macbeth starts a slow, hesi-
tant and nervous walk towards the king, so that he reaches the king as Lady
Macbeth says 'He is about it', and he then stabs him. Lady Macbeth mimes out
her actions to the words read out by the readers, which turns out to be a very
skilled performance, requiring her to turn, to point and to react in just the right
way on every line. Meanwhile, every time she mentions a noise, the sound effects
team have already made the right one, right on cue. The tense atmosphere builds
up. Macbeth times his walk back to her to coincide with the line 'My husband!',
and the sound effects group continue to make their contribution. They have the
job of saying the words of the people Macbeth has heard calling out in their
sleep, so more voices are added to the overall impression. They do 'Murder!' and
'God bless us!' particularly impressively, but they still have a lot of words to say
a bit later. Lady Macbeth becomes impatient with her husband, and tells me
later that she was getting angry with him for being pathetic ('I felt like shaking
him, Miss'), and then eventually she goes back to the bedchamber and smears
the grooms with blood. She hasn't got much time, just the seven lines that
Macbeth mimes to, and then returns to him, while the knocking has been
starting and becoming insistent and loud, and Lady Macbeth hurries him off to
wash his hands and get on his nightgown, while he, the mime actor, himself says
out loud the last two lines of the scene, to emphasize that it is Macbeth himself
coming to this appalling realization of what he has done.

The pupils also perform the earlier scenes which we have worked on, and do
Act II, scene 2 really well at the performance. Unfortunately, few of the audience seem to understand Shakespeare, and their teacher tells me afterwards that
people thought she was mad to try *Macbeth* with such young pupils. We both
disagree with this, and feel that the class did really well, and with such enthusiasm! They are so pleased with themselves, and I am pleased with them because
they have shown yet again that Shakespeare is accessible to anyone, even if that
particular audience was unreceptive. I am also pleased that we devised ways of
involving everyone in the class in the presentation, and feel that we did in fact
deconstruct that scene in some ways, and made a new thing of it.

We still have a lot of the play to go, but unfortunately time has run out. I do
Banquo's death in another school, and Lady Macbeth's sleepwalking in a further
school, but these were both secondary schools. The two classes in that primary
school never did find out what happened to Macbeth and Lady Macbeth, but if
their interest has been aroused before they are 11, who knows what can happen
when they are 16?

Methods used in this work

It might be useful briefly to recapitulate the methods I used:

1 Problem-solving, with objects used as a stimulus, leading to story-writing.
2 For all active work, some warm-up and concentration exercises before starting
   work on the text.

3 Allocating single lines to individual pupils, who say them in many different ways including whispering, shouting.

4 Saying lines while running, miming, speaking round in the circle, playing games with them.

5 Repeating lines read out by teacher, 'showing' them by physical actions.

6 Working out the events and emotions of a scene by responding to 30 single lines presented on cards, reading and working together in groups.

7 Teacher narrating parts of the story without the use of anyone else's version, using the narrative in the script.

8 Learning lines to put together for a whole class effort.

9 Teacher talking pupils into a scene while they listen with eyes closed.

10 Improvising to set a scene, involving the whole class together.

11 Miming actions to words read by group of readers.

12 Using and making sound effects, derived from the script.

13 Written work including stories and poems about witches, Macbeth's letter home to his wife, the murder of Duncan.

10 Shakespeare in the secondary classroom

This chapter contains accounts of classroom work done on several of the plays with year groups ranging from year 7 to years 12 and 13 in several different schools. In providing this I hope to show how the methods I described in Chapter 9 in the primary classroom can be extended and developed, and how some first steps towards a deconstructive approach can be taken. I feel that I need to make clear that while this work was being done I was conscious of a contradiction being continuously set up in my own thinking: I realized that it is impossible to experience a deconstructive process before you have some degree of familiarity with the text to be deconstructed. And yet, how is this familiarity to be gained, in relation to what critical processes and stance, with what level of ideological awareness? It is clearly not possible to experience a text, even for the first time, in a *neutral* way, and particularly not a Shakespeare text: if nothing else, it carries with it for pupils the kind of class connotations that my work was at pains to dispel. There is, and was, no single answer: the teacher has to recognize that whatever approach is used has been *chosen*, from a number of possibilities, and the very act of choosing confirms the teacher, inevitably, in the role of authority. The least controlled and predetermined classroom interactions still depend on the teacher having decided to set them in motion: the 'let's see what happens to this bit of the text if we do this with it' approach depends on the teacher having selected the bit of text, and already having recognized that it can yield up plural meanings.

The challenges facing me with all this work, and facing any teacher starting work on Shakespeare for the first time, were first, to locate each exploration of the text within a graspable framework which at this level is most appropriately supplied by the narratives of the text; second, to find non-threatening ways of speaking the words and understanding the language; and third, to find ways of engaging the active involvement of the whole class. I had to recognize that whatever approach I chose would shape pupils' perceptions of the text quite powerfully, and I had to accept that responsibility. Only with older students who have already become familiar with the text with their own class teacher did I feel that anything like a deconstructive approach was possible, and then the key question was whether the work was deconstructing the text itself (if there is such a thing), or deconstructing the construction the teacher had already put on it.

I will write these accounts in the same way as in Chapter 9, each one dealing with only one aspect of the classroom work experienced by the pupils, so that by taking all the accounts together, the reader can form a full picture of the variety of possible approaches. They include work done on *King Lear* with a year 7 class, *The Tempest* with a year 8 class, *Macbeth* with a year 9 class, *The Merchant of Venice* with a year 10 class, *Romeo and Juliet* and *Macbeth* with year 11 classes. Each of these classes was in a different school, and I worked with them for varying lengths of time. An important factor in this work which I recognized very quickly was that an outside teacher has certain advantages over the normal class teacher; she is able to treat the situation without preconceptions and is therefore regarded by the pupils as neutral and trustable. It may be more difficult for the class to accept that their established class teacher has suddenly changed tack and reorganized teaching style and classroom layout in order to launch into new ways with the texts. Of course, it can be done, but teachers need the confidence to do it.

Work on *King Lear* with a year 7 class

The teacher has chosen this text because she knows it, and I decide to start with a problem-solving approach. The pupils are given two sheets each, one a map of England, the other a set of statements about Lear: there is a king who has decided to give up the kingship because he is growing very old; he has three daughters, two of whom are married; the youngest unmarried daughter is the one he loves best; two suitors are at the court seeking to marry this youngest daughter. What will he do with his kingdom? Pupils work on this in groups, getting very involved in working out ideas. We share ideas after ten minutes, writing them on the board. They seem to think Lear will divide up the kingdom, but have not yet decided how. They go back to thinking about this. After another five minutes they come up with the idea of a test, and we then think about what the king would be testing them for. Lots of ideas offered here, many focusing on suitability for being a ruler, which we also need to think about, some to do with strength, some to do with intelligence. Each group is then asked to work out the test they think most likely, and to report back to the class with their proposal. One group gets close to the actual test, another group includes questions about how the daughters will treat Lear after he has abdicated. The pupils are then asked to think about dividing up the map, according to their own decision: if Lear wanted to be fair, how could he divide up a land so varied in its nature, with mountains as well as fertile plains, rivers as well as heaths? The pupils find this difficult, never having thought about land in this way before. We need to think about this as well, so I ask them to think about what is needed to keep life going, as basic necessities, and they grasp this well. They then see how to look at the land – near a river you can grow crops, in the mountains you cannot, and so on. Already two of the informing ideas of the play are being thought about: the father and the daughters, and the concept of necessity. The teacher says that they will write their own story of what happens when the king divides up his land, with the test he devised, before the next session.

We listen to these stories next time, and decide which test we think most likely. Then we make a circle of chairs, and I give them each a copy of part of Act I, scene 1 of the script from Lear's 'Meantime we shall express our darker purpose' to his 'thou my sometime daughter', and we read in turn, one sentence each, to find out what the test really was, and what happened. The pupils are really involved with this, and even though they do not understand all the words, they are not frightened by the reading as they only have short bits to do. At the end of the reading I ask if anyone can say what they think has been going on. There are several suggestions, and it is clear they have grasped the basic situation, and one girl already does not trust what Goneril said. We read round the group again, this time ready to say one word from what we have read which we think is an important word, so the first reader reads out 'Meantime we shall express our darker purpose' and selects the word 'darker', and so we go round the group. I ask each pupil to say their single word round the group in turn again; the words they have chosen point up the contradictions in the scene, between person and person, and expectation and expectation. We hear all the key words one after the other, and I ask the class what ideas they have of the people in this scene now. What did they think of the test? They thought it was silly, asking for trouble, and we talk in turn round the group about how we would react if our parents demanded a declaration of love. The consensus is that your parents ought to know already that you love them, they should not need to be told. We finish with another reading of the script, so by now they have heard it three times and are becoming familiar with it.

For the next session I have devised a kind of game. I want them to see in physical terms what Lear has done, so I have written out on 30 cards all the words spoken by Lear and his daughters connected with these exchanges of power, with the speaker's name on the back of the card. We choose a volunteer Lear, Goneril, Regan and Cordelia, who sit in the middle of the circle. Each pupil in the circle is given one or more of the cards. I ask the pupils in turn to go up to the relevant character in the middle and give them their card, so for instance a pupil holding a card with the words 'dearer than eyesight' goes up to Goneril and has to say 'I give you, Goneril, the words "dearer than eyesight"', and then returns to his place. The cards have been distributed completely at random, so there is no sequence about this, but the pupils are saying the words, saying the names, and participating in a little ritualized exchange which commands their complete involvement. When all the cards have been given to the characters in the middle, they have to enact their own exchanges, thus Lear gives to Goneril 'shadowy forests', 'champains riched' and so on, while she gives him 'Dearer than space', 'dearer than liberty' and so on. The pupils are quite startled when the only card Cordelia gives is the word 'nothing' and the only one she receives is 'nothing'. When the exchanges are complete, I ask the pupils who has come out of this best. They can all see that it is Goneril and Regan, and they also see that what Lear has is worthless, it is just words with no substance. They begin to see how untrustworthy words are.

By now the pupils are becoming very familiar with this part of the scene, and in later sessions we go on to work on other scenes, using all the speaking strategies which I described in Chapter 9, shouting, whispering, running about saying words. Before we start work each session we have a recapitulation round the circle, each pupil being expected to add something to what we know of the story so far, so there is a continual reinforcement of the narrative framework. There is no time to do the whole play, but in the last session, we work hard on Lear's speech 'Blow winds and crack your cheeks'. We are able to use the drama theatre for this, which allows us to shout and scream without disturbing anyone. The pupils have a line each to begin with, and first we say the lines, then we try shouting the lines, then we add in sound effects having identified the sounds of the storm, and say the speech with marvellous accompanying noises, and great excitement and enjoyment. These pupils have not done all of *King Lear* but they have learnt that Shakespeare is enjoyable.

Work on *The Tempest* with a year 8 class

I decide to set up a similar problem-solving exercise for the pupils with this text, involving some thinking about a desert island and these people who are living on it: How did a man and his 13-year-old daughter come to be living there? Where is her mother? How did he take the island over from Caliban? How has he become the master of Ariel? The work follows the pattern of other challenges like this, with story-writing and illustrations of their own as immediate outcomes. We start work in earnest on Act I, scene 1, in the carpeted hall of the school, where we have a great deal of space. I follow the previous formula of allocating the lines I have already selected out of the scene, to do with the danger, the fear and the threats, and we try them out, working out what is going on, and then we really activate it. The pupils have learnt their lines now, and I divide them into two groups, one at each end of the hall. It does not matter what their lines are for this. Then they run in turn shouting out their lines in the correct order from one group to the other, so there is always one person running across the space from one end of the hall or the other. When we have done this, with great energy and vocal strength, we use the words to make a sinking ship. In the order of their lines they run into the middle of the room shouting their lines as they do so and form a compact shape of intertwined bodies, trying to keep their balance as the ship tosses on the wild waves. When they are all on board, I go round tapping them on the shoulder at random, their signal to fall off the ship, shouting out their line in despair, and to lie drowned on the floor. The pupils think this is marvellous, and have also managed to participate in something which conveyed a powerful sense of fear and danger.

I have to do a lot of narrative work in subsequent sessions to make this all make sense, and we also read a cut version of Prospero's long story about himself, in the usual way. We investigate Caliban, considering what he says about the island and Prospero's treatment of him when he first arrived, reading and saying his words, and deciding what we think of his present position. I want them to begin to see that his position is not inevitable, to see the other side of Prospero's colonization. They work on Ariel's speech describing how he 'flamed amazement', with actions showing the words. We do some choral work on Ariel's song 'Full fathom five' as part of investigating Ferdinand. I am amazed at what pupils will do when they are involved: for this song we split the lines, we have words repeated, we have lines echoed, and then we add in the bell ringing the knell, sounding between lines, and then more fully at the end. By the end of this session we have achieved some quite surprising effects, which impress us all. Before my time comes to an end in this school we have a chance to find out who the people are in the ship, and to decide what we think Prospero should do with them. At this stage, the pupils are all for revenge: if I had longer with them I would investigate Prospero's behaviour in Milan, his performance as a ruler of a city, allowing the class to challenge Prospero's favourable view of himself as victim and to think about what the responsibilities of a power-holder should be, and whether they think there should be power-holders. However, when I leave we all feel that something very worthwhile has been achieved, and these pupils have really enjoyed their sessions, and have all joined in very energetically. This class was very mixed ethnically, and in other teaching situations was found to be difficult, but their class teacher worked very well with them, and they responded with huge enthusiasm to all the work we did.

Work on *Macbeth* with a year 9 class

Much of the work I do with this group in the two sessions I am with them is a shortened version of what I did in the primary school, but I do a further scene with them. They already know the play to some extent, so I do not have the problem of conveying the story of it. We work on the death of Banquo, looking at Act III, scene 3 in great detail. Once we have sorted out the location and personae of the scene, I put them into groups of five, and ask them to produce a freeze frame, a snapshot to show what it is about. They need to read the scene again, to work on its meanings and its indications of physical relationships, its indications of movement, and gradually they put their ideas together. Their teacher and I move about the hall helping where needed, but mainly asking questions. I try to avoid answering questions, and constantly refocus them back onto the script, which is one of the easier parts of the play. I wonder what they will see as the most important moment of the scene: the death of Banquo or the escape of Fleance? and what will they make of the third murderer who has been told to join them? When we show the tableaux, I tell the pupils to walk round each one, looking closely at it. When the tableau is dissolved they can ask questions about it: Why were they in the positions they were in? What were they thinking? What did they expect to happen next? The tableaux divide fairly equally between those showing the murder being committed, with Fleance just turning to run, and those after the murder with Fleance some way off and the murderers realizing they have lost him. I ask one Fleance why he is so far away from his father – why didn't he try to help? I ask another one what he is thinking as he looks over his shoulder at his dying father? We ask the murderers what they are thinking, what they think will happen to them? The pupils justify their positions, and begin to see how the same words on the page can result in very different physicalization. I am pleased with this work, and see that it would have been possible with year 8 pupils, too, although more difficult for primary pupils. Only with pupils who can read sufficiently well can I do work like this. I notice the differences shown by this class because they know the play: it is harder for them to discount the perceptions they have already formed, harder for them to relax, as though the previous experience of the text has already constrained them into a certain set of relationships with it.

Work on *The Merchant of Venice* with year 10 pupils

In my preparatory reading of this text, I decided that there were two things in particular that I wanted to do with it: to open up the whole position of Shylock for investigation, and show the centrality of money in relation to the women as well as the men. At the same time the pupils will need to be given the story in one way or another, as they do not know the play at all. I devise a similar problem-solving exercise to the earlier ones, about Portia's father ensuring that she marries the right kind of man by leaving particular conditions set down in his will. The questions to be answered are: What are the conditions? And how can the dead father ensure that they are carried out? They work in groups discussing this, suggesting ideas, we share ideas using the board to note them on, and they go away to write their own narrative version of this. They immediately relate to the framework presented to them as a fairy story, and their own writing is couched in the fairy-tale formulae. I hope they will come close to what actually happens in the text, but while they produce some well-written stories, they do not think up the idea of a choice between three caskets. In the next session we work on these caskets, by having three suitably coloured boxes in the classroom, and the three inscriptions from the text in large letters pinned on the walls. I put the pupils into groups, and ask them to do three things, having explained that these caskets are the method of choice laid down by Portia's father: first, to decide which is the winning casket; second, to decide which inscription goes with which casket; and third, to make up their own message to go inside each casket, along with the reward inside the winning one and the punishment inside the losing ones. I am surprised that they find the inscriptions as difficult to place as they do, although they do very well with the contents of the caskets, making up some horrible punishments for the losers. Surprisingly, they do not all think the lead casket should be the winner, but opt instead for a kind of double bind, outwitting any suitor who thinks he'll win by appearing to be humble. They show great astuteness with these contents.

We play a game between the groups, where each individual from one group has to choose a casket from another group's arrangement, read the message inside, and not divulge the answer until the whole group has had a turn and then two more groups work together and so on. Each individual has to use a formula of words, to bring some semblance of a ritual to the whole affair, saying, 'My name is . . . and I have come to seek the hand of Portia in marriage' and the spokesperson for the casket group says, 'Welcome . . . Do you understand the conditions of the test?' to which the suitor replies, 'I do.' The spokesperson asks, 'Are you prepared to abide by the rules, and to comply with what you find in the casket of your choice?' to which the suitor should reply 'I am', and the spokesperson then says, 'You may proceed to make your choice'. When all the suitors from one group have chosen and read their messages, they are either told, '—— (name of suitor), you have made the correct choice of casket and you have won the hand of Portia in marriage. Place your hand on the casket and swear that you will stay with her and care for her for the rest of your lives', or ' . . . you have made the incorrect choice of casket. You have sworn to abide by the conditions laid down, and are therefore condemned/ordered to . . . (reads out the punishment from the chosen casket). Place your hand on the casket and swear that you will carry out the terms of your punishment'. The suitor then has to swear appropriately.

What I want this game to achieve is to formalize and ritualize an exchange, to alert the pupils to the significance of swearing to do something by placing your hand on a symbolic object, and to the whole idea of making bargains, giving your word. In later work on the text I shall want to go back to this idea in examining Shylock's adherence to his bond, although unfortunately I do not have the time in this school. The pupils in their decisions about the caskets have already made the link between Portia and money.

For Shylock, I devise a way into his story and relationships which can show the pupils that everyone involved with money and merchant-venturing is compromised. In the next sessions we sit in the circle of chairs, and work on parts of the text, using a photocopied sheet which has three extracts from Antonio in Act I, scene 1, two extracts from Bassanio in the same scene, and Shylock's speech 'How like a fawning publican he looks' from the next scene. The pupils are asked to read the extracts round the group, play about with the words, pick one word out of their line, discuss what is going on, and then attempt to put the extracts in the right order. They are asked for their verdict on Bassanio at this stage. Later we spend a whole session on Shylock's speech 'Signor Antonio, many a time and oft/on the Rialto you have rated me', activating the words, showing them, shouting them and learning one line each. I ask them what they think of Shylock: should he lend money to Antonio? Opinions vary, but they all feel angry on his behalf. Later work again looks at what is said about Shylock in the play, and by whom. We use photocopied sheets with all the relevant extracts, and work out from them who is most against Shylock, who is most 'racist', as the pupils say. Surprisingly, it is Gratiano, so they now have a point of view of him which will help them challenge the text's apparent condoning of the treatment of Shylock.

To physicalize perceptions about Antonio, Bassanio and Shylock, we play another game. Each group of three pupils is given a handful of old coins which they distribute equally between them. There is an Antonio, a Bassanio and a Shylock in each group, and on the basis of the information on the first photocopied sheet we used, they have to dispose of their coins in a suitable fashion. When they see that neither Antonio nor Bassanio have any left at all, but that Shylock still has all his money, they voice their disapproval of Antonio and Bassanio, and find themselves much more in favour of Shylock than of the other two. The game establishes an idea of Shylock for the pupils, which is very vigorously expressed when they are invited to consider what kind of penalty Shylock might exact from Antonio on non-payment of the three thousand ducats. Their suggestions are far more violent than Shakespeare's! All the work devised for this class has to take account of the rather small classroom we are in, and the impossibility of using any bigger space. It is also difficult to sit in a circle, so I do not feel that the work has enhanced any sense of class identity.

Work on *Macbeth* with a year 11 class

With this class I do a piece of work on the text which I have not tried before and I am keen to see what happens. We have already done a lot of work on parts of the text, the storyline is familiar to them, and they have participated as a whole group in a lot of physicalizing and speaking of the text. For this one piece of work I give them a sheet with the following speeches on it:

LADY MACBETH:

Come, you spirits
That tend on mortal thoughts, unsex me here
And fill me from the crown to the toe top-full
Of direst cruelty. Make thick my blood;
Stop up the access and passage to remorse,
That no compunctious visitings of nature
Shake my fell purpose, nor keep peace between
The effect and it. Come to my woman's breasts
And take my milk for gall, you murdering ministers,
Wherever in your sightless substances,
You wait on nature's mischief. Come, thick night,
And pall thee in the dunnest smoke of hell,
That my keen knife see not the wound it makes,
Nor heaven peep through the blanket of the dark
To cry, 'Hold, hold!'

MACBETH:

> Come, seeling night,
> Scarf up the tender eye of pitiful day,
> And with thy bloody and invisible hand
> Cancel and tear to pieces that great bond
> Which keeps me pale. Light thickens
> And the crow makes wing to the rooky wood;
> Good things of day begin to droop and drowse,
> Whiles night's black agents to their preys do rouse.
> Thou marvell'st at my words; but hold thee still.
> Things bad begun make strong themselves by ill.

We read the speeches round in the circle, and focus on the atmosphere produced by the words, using the same techniques as already described. When I feel that the students are familiar with the sound and the meaning of these speeches, I ask them in pairs to put the two speeches together in any way they like and decide how they are going to read out the result. The only stipulation is that they must say all the words at least once, but they can repeat as much as they like. When they come to read out what they have done, the effect is quite electrifying. With one of the readings I find the hairs standing up along the back of my neck, and shivers down my spine, and I know the play! Another teacher watching the lesson feels the same effect, although I do not think the students quite realize what they have achieved. However, they have seen what you can do with parts of the text, and that marrying two speeches together like this produces other effects and intensified meanings. It also puts Lady Macbeth on a par with Macbeth, powerfully synthesizing their parallel invocations. This work would have been impossible in the primary classroom but here it works really well.

Work on *Romeo and Juliet* with a year 11 class

I want to describe three approaches used here, none of which have yet been mentioned in these practical chapters. The first is a way of getting into the narrative situation of the play quickly. I was working to a tight schedule with this class, because the work generated by the lessons was intended for their GCSE folders, so we needed to know the situation immediately. I did not want to tell them myself, or read out another narrative version, so I devised the following: I took as my standpoint the point of the play after the first street fight, and after Paris has made his offer of marriage to Capulet. I wrote descriptions of ten characters in the play, as they appear up to that moment, as though I was addressing them, thus: 'You are the Prince of Verona, and you are becoming increasingly angry at the brawling in the streets caused by the Capulets' and the Montagues' feud. You realize you should have put a stop to it years ago. Your citizens do not automatically listen to you when you appear in the street. You have several kinsmen (relatives), among them Mercutio.' This simplified de-lineation of the Prince is replicated in all the other descriptions, of Capulet,

Lady Capulet, the Nurse, Juliet, Romeo, Tybalt, Benvolio, Mercutio and Friar Lawrence. The students are asked to sit in groups of five, and are given individually within their group two of these descriptions. I ask them to read them to themselves, and then, saying who they are, to tell the rest of the group about themselves, without reading aloud from the paper. The first characters to do this feel a bit silly, but gradually as more information is added to each group's store, they recognize connections and relationships between the characters. We come together as a class when they have finished, and I ask each person who was one of the characters, say all the Juliets, to tell us about herself, making sure that they each contribute something. In this way the whole experience is shared and we all know the basic situation. This activity also breaks down a few gender expectations, because the papers were given out at random, and several boys have female characters and vice versa.

Their teacher tells me some weeks later how well they remember the relationships of the characters from this introductory work and is very pleased. At a much later session, we work on Capulet threatening Juliet. We all have a copy of Capulet's speech from Act III, scene 5, 'God's bread it makes me mad', and we have already read it round the group several times. Now we have the gist of it, and we are going to make it really unpleasant. I ask for a courageous volunteer to stand in the middle of the circle. We are all standing now, not sitting. The first volunteer is a boy. I allocate lines round the group, so each person has one bit to say, and ask them to learn it. Then I ask them to go up to the volunteer Juliet in the middle, and say their line as angrily as they can, and as they return to their place in the circle, the next person is already shouting at her, so there is an unbroken sound of fury coming from the group. This does not work the first time, because they have not yet learnt their lines, and they are not used to shouting – we are in a classroom surrounded by other classrooms. The second time it begins to sound more threatening, and then for the third time I say that they can make some physical contact with 'Juliet' in the middle, but not violently so; a push, maybe, to indicate their anger. This really works, and even becomes quite unpleasant. I ask Juliet how he feels, and he says it was very scary, he did not like it. They have experienced the energy and anger contained in those words, and in spite of our cramped working conditions, they have really begun to let go. They have begun to feel the situation of Juliet, and of any young person in a family situation being bullied by a parent. They think Capulet is mad and do not like him at all. They go on to write some very good folder pieces about Juliet and her parents. In future work Capulet's point of view must be examined.

We conclude our work on the text with a mourning exercise for Juliet. I use the lines from Act IV, scene 5, where Juliet is found apparently dead. We are sitting in the circle, and each student has a copy of the scene in its entirety. I hope we can do something with the scene to allow it the weight it should have, and to let it operate as a real mourning scene for Juliet. It is repetitive, and full of heavy sounds, can only be spoken slowly, and the profusion of 'O's in it usually produces giggles. I introduce it to them, and we read it round the circle, roughly one line each, and then we focus on the scene from the end of the Nurse's first speech 'Alas, alas! Help, help!'. The students are trying very hard, but this is not easy. I have brought some music by John Dowland, the 'Lachrymae', to the session, and now I tell the students that while they read I am going to have it playing quietly in the background. There is an immediate change in the atmosphere, the music imposing a sadness, and a poignancy. When we have finished reading the words for the third time, I ask them to choose one line each from the scene which they feel expresses their grief at Juliet's death. I play the music again, asking them to say their chosen line, with bowed head. Some lines are repeated, which adds to the elegiac mood. I have to judge whether they are ready for the next step. This is an exercise that I have participated in myself, and when everyone involved is serious about it, it can be unbearably moving. If the students are not quite ready for it, it will not work. I decide to trust them. I ask for one person to lie on the floor, to be the dead Juliet. With the music playing again, we each in turn go up to Juliet, kneel down and say our line, making any gesture we feel like making, maybe touching her, maybe hiding our eyes, whatever seems suitable. We all take this quite seriously. I am glad I decided to do it with the class, some of them seem quite subdued afterwards.

I have indicated in the foregoing accounts where I found difficulties, and where ideas did not work. I must also make clear that most of this work was devised for ordinary classrooms. It is quite possible to energize work on the texts even in the confined space afforded by a classroom, and although a hall or drama studio is very welcome, it is not a *sine qua non*. Some of the work might well look like the head-on approach which I discussed earlier, but none of it is reading round the class in parts, most of it is away from desks, and designed to encourage collaboration. I was surprised, for example, to discover how static are the relationships in most classes, and how pupils do not always know each other's names if they are not friends. It became very clear how many learning opportunities are denied to pupils by keeping them fixed in their desks, and how unidirectional the communications in the classroom remain, between teacher at the front, and pupils in desks facing the front. The cross-class interactions produced in this kind of one-way arrangement, which could be used so fruitfully, often degenerate into personal chat and non-productive, even negative interactions among students. This work on the Shakespeare texts can exploit all the creativity and energy of classes in highly enjoyable and concentrated ways.

I mentioned the requirements of A level courses in Chapter 8, and have not described any possible work. As will be readily apparent, much of the work I have described here can be adapted for A level. Some concentration on the narrative line would seem appropriate, in view of comments made about A level performance in examinations, for example: 'few candidates had a really commanding knowledge of the chronological narrative of *King Lear*' (AEB Reports of

Examiners, June Examination 1990, AEB, Guildford). Work which focuses on key words and on key thoughts enhances understanding considerably, and examining parts of the text in parallel, such as Hamlet's soliloquies, reveals hitherto hidden significances. Any technique which opens up, challenges, explores, and refuses to accept the text's own privileging of situations and characters is of great value to students. They are able to investigate the significance of absence and silence in a way that is not available to younger pupils, and they deserve to be challenged, both physically and mentally, by the complexities of the Shakespeare text.

Notes

Chapter 1

1 Gary Taylor, *Reinventing Shakespeare*. London, The Hogarth Press (1990). A review in the *Sunday Times*, 21 January 1990, by John Carey, Merton Professor of English Literature at Oxford University, takes issue with Taylor's contention that Shakespeare was not uniquely gifted and that his position was the result of the treatment that had been given him, but ultimately Carey can only repeat that Shakespeare is great because Shakespeare is great.

2 *The Guardian*, 15 September 1990.

3 Jane Austen, *Mansfield Park* [1814], Chapter 34.

4 Ben Jonson (1573–1637), with his 'He was not of an age, but for all time!', is best known, but William Basse (d. 1653), Thomas Fuller (1608–1661) and John Milton (1608–1674) all wrote about Shakespeare in terms of highest praise; Heminge and Condell wrote in their Preface to the first Folio collection of the plays: 'His mind and hand went together, and what he thought, he uttered with that easinesse, that we have scarse received from him a blot in his papers' (*sic*).

5 Anthony Ashley Cooper, Earl of Shaftesbury, *Soliloquy: or, Advice to an Author* (1710).

6 Dionysius Longinus, *On the Sublime*, trans. William Smith (1739), Section XXXIII.

7 H.N. Coleridge (ed.), *Specimens of the Table Talk of the Late Samuel Taylor Coleridge*, 2 vols (1835), (24 June 1827).

8 H.E. Rollins (ed.), *The Letters of John Keats 1814–1821*, 2 vols (1958).

9 'Byron and Shelley on the character of Hamlet', *New Monthly Magazine 29*, (1830).

10 P.P. Howe (ed.), 'Hamlet' in 'Characters of Shakespeare's plays' (1817) in *The Complete Works of William Hazlitt*, 21 vols (1930).

11 A.C. Bradley (1851–1935), *Shakespearean Tragedy. Lectures on Hamlet, Othello, King Lear, Macbeth* (1904). Bradley was Professor of Poetry at Oxford from 1901 to 1906.

12 Austen, *Mansfield Park*, Chapter 34.

13 Sir Walter Raleigh (1861–1922), Professor of English Literature at Oxford from 1904, *Shakespeare* (1907). John Dover Wilson (1881–1969), editor of the *New Cambridge Shakespeare*, most notably author of *What Happens in 'Hamlet'*.

14 George Saintsbury, *A History of Elizabethan Literature* (1887).

15 Algernon Charles Swinburne (1837–1909), *General Introduction to The Comedies,*

Tragedies, Histories and Poems of Shakespeare. Oxford, Oxford University Press (1911).

16 Department of Education and Science *English for Ages 5 to 16* (Cox Report), London, HMSO (1989), whose references to Shakespeare are discussed extensively in Chapter 2. The National Curriculum for English, a statutory obligation for schools, having become law in 1990, divides English into three main Attainment Target areas, Speaking and Listening, Reading, and Writing, which are to be assessed at four Keystages during a pupil's statutory school life, at ages 7, 11, 14 and 16.

17 Aaron Hill (1685–1750), *King Henry the Fifth: OR The Conquest of France by the English* (1723).

18 Charles Dickens (1812–1870), *Great Expectations* [1860], Chapter 31.

19 Charles Dickens, *Nicholas Nickleby* [1839], Chapter 25.

20 Mark Twain (1835–1910), *The Adventures of Huckleberry Finn* [1884], Chapter 21.

Chapter 2

1 Alan Sinfield, 'Give an account of Shakespeare and Education, showing why you think they are effective and what you have appreciated about them. Support your comments with precise references' in J. Dolimore and A. Sinfield, eds, *Political Shakespeare.* Manchester, Manchester University Press (1985).

2 The idea of civilizing the working classes through the elevating effect of the study of English literature was expressed by several theorists and critics in the nineteenth and early twentieth centuries, notably Matthew Arnold (1822–1888), and in the collective wisdom of the *Report of the Departmental Committee of the Teaching of English in England* (Newbolt Report), London, HMSO (1921). See also Brian Doyle, *English and Englishness*, London, Routledge (1989), for an exhaustive discussion of the subject.

3 David Hornbrook, ' "Go play, boy, play": Shakespeare and educational drama' in Graham Holderness, ed., *The Shakespeare Myth.* Manchester, Manchester University Press (1988).

4 Shakespeare Day, an annual commemoration held in elementary schools in the early 20th century, is discussed in the Introduction to Malcolm Evans, *Signifying Nothing.* Brighton, Harvester Press (1986).

5 These O level questions are referred to in Sinfield, 'Give an account', p. 139.

6 Shakespeare always featured on the list of prescribed works, from which choices had to be made, but was never obligatory.

7 Sir Arthur Quiller-Couch (1863–1944) became first Professor of English Literature at Cambridge University in 1912, and was the general editor of J.M. Dent's heavily expurgated school editions of Shakespeare's plays.

8 Terry Eagleton, *Literary Theory: An Introduction.* Oxford, Basil Blackwell (1983), p. 31.

9 Sir Alan Bullock, chairman, *A Language for Life*, London, HMSO (1975), Chapter 9 'Literature', and Chapter 1 'Attitudes to the Teaching of English'.

10 Department of Education and Science, *English from 5 to 16: Curriculum Matters 1.* London, HMSO (1984).

11 Department of Education and Science, *English from 5 to 16: Responses to Curriculum Matters 1.* London, DES (1986).

12 Sir John Kingman, *Report of the Committee of Inquiry into the Teaching of English Language.* London, HMSO (1988), Chapter 2.22.

13 The 'Shakespeare in Schools' project ran from 1986 to 1989. The report on the work undertaken during those years has not yet been published. The work of the project is specifically referred to in DES, *English for Ages 5 to 16* (Cox Report), London, HMSO (1989): 'The *Shakespeare in Schools* Project, at the Cambridge Institute of Education, has shown that secondary pupils of a wide range of abilities can find Shakespeare accessible, meaningful and enjoyable.' Dr Rex Gibson has since undertaken the editorship of a new Cambridge edition of the plays, which will incorporate page-by-page suggestions for using much of the practical active work of the project.

14 I am indebted to Professor Cox for giving this interview in July 1990 and making it so enjoyable.

15 Schools Examination and Assessment Council, *GCSE Criteria for English, Applicable to Examinations in and from 1994*. London, HMSO (1990), para. 3.6.

16 The Cox Report, Chapter 7.16, indicates measures of disagreement, including 'those who deny his universality', and 'almost everyone agrees that his work should be represented in a National Curriculum.'

Chapter 3

1 DES, *English for Ages 5 to 16* (Cox Report). London, HMSO (1989).

2 Robert McCrum, William Cran and Robert MacNeil, *The Story of English*. Viking (1986); Raymond Williams, *The Long Revolution*. London, Penguin (1961); David Crystal, *The Cambridge Encyclopaedia of Language*. Cambridge, Cambridge University Press (1987).

3 In connection with the ideological purposes which can be discerned behind these statements, it is instructive to consider demands for changes in the National Curriculum History proposals, which would anchor the teaching of History much more firmly into overtly nationalistic patterns. In March 1991, the then Secretary of State for Education, Kenneth Clarke, imposed a 20-year rule on the teaching of History; no events more recent than 20 years earlier may be taught in schools in the maintained sector of the education system, although schools in the private sector are free to do as they please.

4 Terry Eagleton, *Literary Theory: An Introduction*. Oxford, Basil Blackwell (1983).

5 Alan Sinfield, 'Give an account of Shakespeare and Education, showing why you think they are effective and what you have appreciated about them. Support your comments with precise references' in J. Dollimore and A. Sinfield, eds, *Political Shakespeare*. Manchester, Manchester University Press (1985).

6 Sir Alan Bullock, *A Language For Life*. London, HMSO (1975), Chapter 9, p. 131.

7 Sir John Kingman, *Report of the Committee of Inquiry into the Teaching of English Language*. London, HMSO (1988), para. 2.25.

8 See David Hornbrook, ' "Go play, boy, play": Shakespeare and educational drama' in Graham Holderness, ed., *The Shakespeare Myth*. Manchester, Manchester University Press (1988).

9 Eagleton, *Literary Theory*.

10 W. Moelwyn Merchant, ed., *The Merchant of Venice*, Harmondsworth, Penguin (1967), p. 60.

11 Ibid., p. 7

12 Ibid., p. 50

13 Sinfield, 'Give an account'.
14 Alessandro Serpieri, 'Reading the signs: towards a semiotics of Shakespearean drama' in John Drakakis, ed., *Alternative Shakespeares*. London, Methuen (1985).
15 Eagleton, *Literary Theory*.
16 Raymond Williams, *Keywords*. London, Fontana (1976).
17 Malcolm Evans, *Signifying Nothing*. Brighton, Harvester Press (1986), p. 8.

Chapter 4

1 These examination boards are currently adapting to many challenges, not least the growing popularity of open text and coursework A levels, the uncertainties about the whole future of A levels, and the possibilities of radical changes in A level courses and university entrance requirements.
2 There is a useful analysis and discussion of the significance and influence of these linguists and others in Catherine Belsey, *Critical Practice*. London, Methuen (1980).
3 I am unable to find the precise reference to this particular event during Olivier's season at Elsinore. I have read an account of how one performance of *Hamlet* had to be done in a hurried and improvised manner with no extra lighting and minimal staging because of some mishap; the performance was overwhelming and electrifying, energized by the sense of emergency.
4 Saxo Grammaticus, the thirteenth-century Danish historian who wrote down the story of *Hamlet*, partly in Latin. It seems likely that only with the building of Kronberg castle in the sixteenth century did Elsinore (Helsingør) come to be a known place name abroad beyond its function as a port.
5 Examples from JMB Theatre Studies for 1983: 'What interpretation of *Hamlet* reflects most accurately your own feelings about the play and why? You may refer to any productions you have seen or read about'; and ' "A lonely, pure, noble and most moral nature without the strength of nerve which forms a hero, sinks beneath a burden which it cannot bear." Do you agree with Goethe's estimate of Hamlet's role?' True, the words 'play', 'productions' and 'role' are used, but no active recreation of the text is allowed.
6 Walsall LEA still retains two grammar schools: the teachers responding to the questionnaire were all in 'creamed-off' comprehensive schools.
7 The Royal Shakespeare Theatre Education Department runs in-service courses for teachers, as well as workshops and courses for pupils, and has greatly expanded its range of operations in the past few years.
8 See DES, *English for Ages 5 to 16* (Cox Report). London, HMSO (1989), para. 7.16.

Chapter 5

1 These editions are listed in the References section.
2 Charles Connell, *They Gave us Shakespeare*. Stocksfield, Oriel Press (1982). Connell points out: 'The rough material they [Heminge and Condell] had to work on comprised old prompt books ... , quarto editions already printed, some of which were in a deplorable condition; copies that had been made of Shakespeare's own manuscripts; the author's "foul papers"; assembled texts or copies put together from actors' memorised parts'.
3 This account was given during the RSC/Folger Shakespeare Library joint course for teachers in July/August 1990, by Peter Blayney, Folger Library research scholar.

4 Steven Urkowitz, teacher/participant on the above course, now head of the Shakespeare Institute, CUNY Graduate Center, New York.
5 There is a useful chapter on the textual and editorial problems thrown up by the differences in punctuation between the Quarto and Folio versions of some of the texts in G.B. Harrison, *Introducing Shakespeare*, Harmondsworth, Penguin (1939).
6 Frankie Rubinstein, *A Dictionary of Shakespeare's Sexual Puns and their Significance.* Basingstoke, Macmillan Press (1989).

Chapter 6

1 Board of Education, *Consultative Committee on Secondary Education Report with Special Reference to Grammar Schools and Technical High Schools* (Spens Report). London, HMSO (1938).
2 F.R. Leavis and D. Thompson, *Culture and Environment*. London, Chatto and Windus (1933).
3 L. Masterman, 'Television and the English teacher' in Anthony Adams, ed., *New Directions in English Teaching*. Lewes, Falmer Press (1982).
4 Ministry of Education, *Half our Future: A Report of the Central Advisory Council for Education* (England) (Newsom Report). London, HMSO (1963).
5 G. Murdock and G. Phelps, *Mass Media and the Secondary School*. London, Macmillan (1973).
6 Sir Alan Bullock, chairman, *A Language for Life*. London, HMSO (1975); DES, *English for Ages 5 to 16* (Cox Report). London, HMSO (1989).
7 Bullock Report, para. 22.14.
8 Len Masterman, 'Television and the English teacher'.
9 Cary Bazalgette, ed., *Primary Media Education: A Curriculum Statement*. London, BFI Education Department (1989).
10 Department of Education and Science, *English in the National Curriculum*, no. 2, London, HMSO (1990).
11 Duncan Graham, chairman, *Non-Statutory Guidance: English*. York, National Curriculum Council (1990).
12 Masterman, 'Television and the English teacher'.
13 Jonathan Miller, *Subsequent Performances*. London, Faber and Faber (1986), Part 1, p. 66.
14 The BBC transmitted a production of *Julius Caesar* in 1938, a stage production of *Twelfth Night* in 1938, and a full-dress studio production of *The Tempest* in 1939.
15 Miller, *Subsequent Performances*.
16 Cedric Messina, quoted in a preface to the BBC editions of the plays he had produced, *The BBC-TV Shakespeare*, which used the Alexander texts of 1951.
17 Gary Waller, 'Decentering the Bard' in J.C. Bulman and H.R. Coursen, eds, *Shakespeare on Television*, Hanover, NH, University Press of New England (1988).
18 Jonathan Miller, interviewed in Graham Holderness, ed., *The Shakespeare Myth*. Manchester, Manchester University Press (1988).
19 Graham Holderness, 'Boxing the Bard: Shakespeare and television' in Holderness, *The Shakespeare Myth*.
20 Susan Willis, 'The British Shakespeare Series' in Bulman and Coursen, *Shakespeare on Television*.
21 Roman Polanski's film version of *Macbeth* made in 1971.

Chapter 7

1 George Brandes (1895) quoted in John Russell Brown, ed., *Shakespeare: Much Ado About Nothing and As You Like It*. Basingstoke, Macmillan (1979).
2 R.A. Foakes, ed., *Much Ado About Nothing*, Harmondsworth Penguin, (1968).
3 Foakes, Introduction, in ibid.
4 Ann Thompson, 'The warrant of womanhood: Shakespeare and feminist criticism' in Graham Holderness, ed., *The Shakespeare Myth*. Manchester, Manchester University Press (1988).
5 Kathleen McLuskie, 'The patriarchal bard: feminist criticism and Shakespeare' in Jonathan Dollimore and Alan Sinfield, eds, *Political Shakespeare*. Manchester, Manchester University Press (1985).
6 G.K. Hunter, ed., *Macbeth*. Harmondsworth, Penguin (1967).
7 McLuskie, 'The patriarchal bard'.
8 Catherine Belsey, 'Disrupting sexual difference: meaning and gender in the comedies' in John Drakakis, ed., *Alternative Shakespeares*. London, Methuen (1985).
9 Foakes, *Much Ado*.
10 The secondary meanings of the words quoted are as follows: 'disdainful', stooping for defecation or fornication; 'haggards', whores; 'entirely', sexually potent, not castrated; 'acquaint', a woman's genitals; 'affection', sexual desire, with emphasis on the buttocks; 'shape', sex organs, male and female; 'rarely', of the rear, the arse, a pederast; '(fair)-faced', buttocks, pudendum; '(ill)-headed', testes or scrotum; 'winds', a flatus; 'truth/true', buttocks or anus; 'virtue', chastity in women, potency, virility in men; 'fashions', to fashion, cut, pun on tail/tale, the rump; 'death', orgasm, 'like/liking', homosexual; 'excellent', lewd, with reference to buttocks and pederasty; 'angry' phallic erection, pregnant. The omitted words are self-evident.
11 McLuskie, 'The patriarchal bard'.
12 Anne Barton, ed., *The Tempest*. Harmondsworth, Penguin (1968).
13 McLuskie, 'The patriarchal bard'.

Chapter 8

1 This account was written by Margaret Brown, Head of English at Weobley Comprehensive School, Herefordshire, and first printed in *Shakespeare in Schools*, no. 11 (Spring 1990).
2 In this connection the sycophantic utterances of Cranmer at the end of *Henry VIII* and the paean to the monarchy spoken by the Chorus at the end of *Henry V* are relevant.
3 Niccolò Machiavelli (1469–1527), quoted in David Thomson, ed., *Political Ideas*. Harmondsworth, Penguin (1966).

References

Adams, Richard and Gould, Gerard (1977) *Into Shakespeare: an Introduction to Shakespeare through Drama*. London, Ward Lock Educational.

Austen, Jane (1966) [1814] *Mansfield Park*. Harmondsworth, Penguin.

Belsey, Catherine (1980) *Critical Practice*. London, Methuen.

Bradley, A.C. (1957) *Shakespearean Tragedy*. London, Macmillan.

Bragg, Melvyn (1984) *Laurence Olivier*. London, Hodder and Stoughton.

Brown, John Russell (1974) *Free Shakespeare*. London, Heinemann Educational.

Brown, John Russell (1979) *Shakespeare: Much Ado About Nothing/As You Like It*. Basingstoke, Macmillan.

Bullock, Sir Alan, chairman (1975) *A Language for Life*. London, HMSO.

Bulman, J.C. and Coursen, H.R. (1988) *Shakespeare on Television*. Hanover, NH, University Press of New England.

Cameron, Deborah (1985) *Feminism and Linguistic Theory*. New York, St Martin's Press.

Connell, Charles (1982) *They Gave us Shakespeare*. Stocksfield, Oriel Press.

Crystal, David (1987) *Cambridge Encyclopaedia of Language*. Cambridge, Cambridge University Press.

Crystal, David (1988) *The English Language*. London, Penguin.

Department of Education and Science (1984) *English from 5 to 16*. Curriculum Matters 1. London, HMSO.

Department of Education and Science (1986) *English from 5 to 16* (2nd edn, incorporating responses). Curriculum Matters 1. London, HMSO.

Department of Education and Science (1989) *English for Ages 5 to 16* (Cox Report). London, HMSO.

Dickens, Charles (1965) [1860] *Great Expectations*. Harmondsworth, Penguin.

Dollimore, Jonathan and Sinfield, Alan, eds (1985) *Political Shakespeare*. Manchester, Manchester University Press.

Doyle, Brian (1989) *English and Englishness*. London, Routledge.

Drakakis, John, ed. (1985) *Alternative Shakespeares*. London, Methuen.

Eagleton, Terry (1983) *Literary Theory: An Introduction*. Oxford, Basil Blackwell.

Eagleton, Terry (1984) *The Function of Criticism*. London, Verso.

Eagleton, Terry (1986) *William Shakespeare*. Oxford, Basil Blackwell.

Edwards, Philip (1987) *Shakespeare: A Writer's Progress*. Oxford, Oxford University Press.

Elsom, John, ed. (1989) *Is Shakespeare Still Our Contemporary?* London, Routledge.

Evans, Malcolm (1986) *Signifying Nothing*. Brighton, Harvester Press.

Fox, Levi (1987) *The Shakespeare Handbook*. Boston, MA, G.K. Hall.

French, Marilyn (1982) *Shakespeare's Division of Experience*. London, Jonathan Cape.

Garfield, Leon (1988) *Shakespeare Stories*. London, Lynx.

Gibson, Rex, ed. (1990) *Secondary School Shakespeare*. Cambridge, Cambridge Institute of Education.

Greer, Germaine (1986) *Shakespeare*. Oxford, Oxford University Press.

Griffith, Peter (1987) *Literary Theory and English Teaching*. Milton Keynes, Open University Press.

Harrison, G.B. (1939) *Introducing Shakespeare*. Harmondsworth, Penguin.

Hawkes, Terence (1986) *That Shakespeherian Rag*. London, Methuen.

Hill, Errol (1984) *Shakespeare in Sable. A History of Black Shakespearean Actors*. Amherst, University of Massachusetts Press.

Holderness, Graham (1988) *The Shakespeare Myth*. Manchester, Manchester University Press.

Johnson, Samuel (1989) *Samuel Johnson on Shakespeare*. London, Penguin.

Kingman, Sir John (1988) *Report of the Committee of Inquiry into the Teaching of English Language*. London, HMSO.

McCrum, Robert, Cran, William and MacNeil, Robert (1986) *The Story of English*. New York, Elizabeth Sifton Books, Viking.

Masterman, Len (1982) 'Television and the English teacher' in Anthony Adams, ed., *New Directions in English Teaching*. Lewes, Falmer Press.

Miller, Jonathan (1986) *Subsequent Performances*. London, Faber and Faber.

O'Brien, Veronica (1982) *Teaching Shakespeare*. London, Edward Arnold.

Parker, Patricia and Hartman, Geoffrey, eds (1985) *Shakespeare and the Question of Theory*. London, Methuen.

Rosen, Betty (1988) *And None of It Was Nonsense*. London, Mary Glasgow Publications.

Rubinstein, Frankie (1989) *A Dictionary of Shakespeare's Sexual Puns and their Significance*. Basingstoke, Macmillan Press.

Rutter, Carol (1989) *Clamorous Voices. Shakespeare's Women Today*. London, Women's Press.

Ryan, Kiernan (1989) *Shakespeare*. Hemel Hempstead, Harvester Wheatsheaf.

Saintsbury, George (1887) *A History of Elizabethan Literature*. London, Macmillan.

Schoenbaum, S. (1979) *Shakespeare, The Globe and The World*. New York, Oxford University Press.

Shakespeare, William. Plays in the following editions:

  The Arden Shakespeare (1964) *King Lear*, ed. Kenneth Muir.

  The Arden Shakespeare (1954) *The Tempest*, ed. Frank Kermode.

  The Illustrated Shakespeare (1989) *Macbeth*, ed. Neil King.

  The Illustrated Shakespeare (1989) *Romeo and Juliet*, ed. Neil King.

  The New Penguin Shakespeare (1967) *Coriolanus*, ed. G.R. Hibbard.

  The New Penguin Shakespeare (1980) *Hamlet*, ed. T.J.B. Spencer; introduction, Anne Barton.

  The New Penguin Shakespeare (1972) *King Lear*, ed. G.K. Hunter.

  The New Penguin Shakespeare (1967) *Macbeth*, ed. G.K. Hunter.

  The New Penguin Shakespeare (1967) *The Merchant of Venice*, ed. W. Moelwyn Merchant.

The New Penguin Shakespeare (1968) *Much Ado About Nothing*. ed. R.A. Foakes.
The New Penguin Shakespeare (1967) *Romeo and Juliet*, ed. T.J.B. Spencer.
The New Penguin Shakespeare (1968) *The Tempest*, ed. Anne Barton.
The New Penguin Shakespeare (1968) *Twelfth Night*, ed. M.M. Mahood.
The New Penguin Shakespeare (1969) *The Winter's Tale*, ed. Ernest Schanzer.
New Swan Shakespeare, Advanced Series (1968) *Hamlet*, ed. Bernard Lott.
Oxford University Press (1911) *The Tragedies, The Histories and Poems, The Comedies*, ed. W.J. Craig.
Taylor, Gary (1990) *Reinventing Shakespeare*. London, The Hogarth Press.
Twain, Mark (1953) *The Adventures of Huckleberry Finn*. Harmondsworth, Penguin.
Wells, Stanley, ed. (1986) *The Cambridge Companion to Shakespeare Studies*. Cambridge, Cambridge University Press.
Williams, Raymond (1961) *The Long Revolution*. London, Penguin.
Williams, Raymond (1976) *Keywords*. London, Fontana.

Index